Living Out
God's Purpose and *Plan*

Living Out
God's Purpose and *Plan*

A Practical Guide to Unlocking Your Potential

by

Williams Ossai

All scripture quotations are taken from New King James Version unless Otherwise indicated

Living Out God's purpose and Plan:
A Practical Guide to Unlocking Your Potential
Copyright © 2018 by Williams Ossai. All rights reserved

All rights reserved. No part of this book may be reproduced in any form or by any electronic or mechanical means including information storage and retrieval systems, without permission in writing from the author. The only exception is by a reviewer, who may quote short excerpts in a review.

Williams Ossai
Visit my website at www.wossai.com
Email: williams.ossai@wossai.com

Printed in the United States of America

Kindle Direct Publishing
ISBN: 9781792032837

Contents

Acknowledgments 11
Introduction 15
Chapter One: Your Responsibility 17
    The Two-Fold Instruction 19
    The Good Part, and the Other Part 20
    The Garden 23
    Found the Garden. What Next? 26
Chapter Two: Your Job Description 29
    Work It 30
    Keeping the Right Attitude at Work 32
    Timing in Work 34
Chapter Three: Secular Work 37
    Be Exemplary 39
    The Waiting Room 41
    Operating by a Different Set of Rules 43
    Necessity – the Mother of Invention 46
    Enjoying Multiple Streams of Income 47
    Remember the Lord Thy God 48
Chapter Four: Ministry Work 51
    Lifestyle 52
    Self-Development 53
    Growing in Grace 56
    The Reward of Labor 57

A Note on Receiving 60
Chapter Five: Keep It **63**
Keep: To Keep Clean and Tidy.. 64
Watch: Provide Security.. 69
Preserve: Protect the Interest 73
Chapter Six: Built by Design **77**
Discovering Purpose 80
Be Useful 82
Designed to Be Self Sufficient 86
Chapter Seven: Acquiring New Skills **91**
Relational Skills... 94
Strength in Unity.. 98
Relational skills in marriage 100
Developing Your Intelligence 104
Practice Maturity... 106
Chapter Eight: Cultivating Your Identity **111**
Lazy! Wicked! Unprofitable!... 114
Good and Faithful... 117
Benefits of Training.. 117
Chapter Nine: Exercise Dominion **123**
Defy the Environment 125
Stay Above...127
Build That Ark 128
Reign with Words...129
Are You Known? 131
The Land Flowing with Milk and Honey...................132
The Door of Opportunity 135
Observing Right Practices 136
What Is in Your Hand?...137
Keep It Real..138
Chapter Ten: Stay Focused....................................... **141**
Recognize Opportunity 145
Wait for The Instruction..147

What Are Your Add-Ons?.. 149
Stay Updated.. 151
Importance of Certification 153
Coaching..154
Have a Succession Plan..156
Be Wary of Dream Killers 158

Chapter Eleven: Phases of Execution............................161
Brooding Phase.. 162
Speaking Phase...165
Forming Phase..170
The Phase of The Breath of Life..................................174
Living Phase..177
Rebuilding the Ruins... 180

Chapter Twelve: Dealing with Delays 185
Delays as a Result of Collaboration 189
Fear-Induced Delay.. 192
Gaining Strength in Periods of Delay 193

Chapter Thirteen: Humility: The Path to Greatness... 197
Paul... 199
Joseph...200
Moses..200
Humility Pays 201
Dealing with Pride as a Minister 203
The conclusion in humility 207

Chapter Fourteen: The Role of Prayer 211
Ministering to the Lord 214
Prayer Makes Power Available 215
The Responsibility of Prayer 218
Prayer of Praise and Thanksgiving.............................221

Conclusion 225

Get Connected 227

Dedication

I dedicate this book to these special people, whose presence in my life, have helped to unlock my potential in writing and made the production of this book a success;

To the Holy Spirit, my number one Mentor

To my wife, my number one fan, for her tireless support

To my children: Onyi, Nonso, Ugo and Purity, for their understanding when daddy needed to work

To Herbert, beloved brother and a great teacher of the word

And to Geraldine, for her exceptional editorial service

Acknowledgments

Writing this book has been an education for me, as well as a journey of discovery and self-awareness. I have been blessed with the rich investments of time, resources, skills, competences, and the support of outstanding men and women.

My deep gratitude and profound thanks go to these very special people for their labor of love in the production of this great book, in no particular order:

Briggs Aroloye, I have benefited immensely from your wise counsel and your unwavering belief in my ability to bless the world through writing.

Captain Eze Chinanu, whose brotherly love and friendship, spanning over 25 years, have helped made my dreams come true.

Ken Akpaidem, for providing me a serene home office for the editing of this book. Your contribution to the success of this project is greatly appreciated.

My little man Ese, your "understanding" ensured the editing went smoothly, and on time.

Management staff of Clark Points Global Systems Limited (Anthony Onyebuenyi, Taiwo Thomas, Oloyede Olaosegba, Amarachi Nnorom, Chinasa Okogbue, Ofu Amechi) for your unreserved support and respect for this great project.

Morgan Gabriel for praying for me and believing in me. Your encouraging words that writing shall serve as my pulpit in spreading the message of the kingdom, spurred me to write this book.

My siblings (Nkechi, Uche, Udoka, Ifeoma, Ebere, Chidi and Chioma), who have greatly contributed in my becoming the person I am today. Your presence and roles have significantly helped in shaping my life.

Okoye Jerome, whose treasured friendship and soul stirring discussions, sharpened my focus to unlock my potential, and author this book amongst many.

Pastor Chris Oyakhilome D.Sc D.D., for your teachings reflected in this book, particularly in the area of prayer.

Rev. (Engr.) Solomon Ani and Rev. (Mrs.) Angela Ani, whose ministerial support, prayers and encouragement, helped me to be self-aware. I appreciate your assistance in the book review.

Oluwaseun Aberuagba, for your unreserved support and benevolence. Your brotherly love is rare.

Otobore Olumoye, you seized every opportunity to reiterate your opinion, that the world needs to hear my messages through writing. Thank you for your encouragement and editorial service.

Bishop Ukaegbu Ogwo, father figure and friend. Thank you for granting me the opportunity and platform, to share my messages online. This has greatly boosted my confidence as a writer and an author. Thank you, sir.

A lot more people were involved in putting this entire project together. I may not have the space requirement, to make individual mention of everyone's role and contribution. You all have my deep appreciation, and profound thanks. God bless you all.

Introduction

Every child of God has a divine mandate for productivity. The very first thing God said to man was to place a demand on him to *"be fruitful and multiply; fill the earth and subdue it; have dominion over the fish of the sea, over the birds of the air, and over every living thing that moves on the earth"* (Genesis 1:28).

As children of God, we are expected to succeed in life. Indeed, some evidently succeed and are applauded as stars. Others succeed without much recognition and applause. Sadly though, a lot of Christians, who love God and serve Him faithfully seem to struggle in different areas of life.

Why? Why are the results and lives of many Christians at variance with the manifold blessings for the man/woman who is in Christ?

The responsibility for the seeming shortfall cannot be attributed to God for we know the sum of His word is truth.

So, wherein lies the problem?

This book is written as a result of a gaping shortfall in the life of the author and his quest for answers from the word of God. Having sought the face of the Lord, God began to show him from the scriptures, principles and strategies to put a definite end to the dilemma of unproductivity.

These principles of productivity have been compiled in this book to steer you into a life of unending productivity and success.

As you read this book, you begin a journey of discovery.

May the Lord speak to your heart as He did to mine thus giving light to these guiding principles which have blessed me and are guaranteed to make tremendous impact in your life.

As you journey through this book, may you discover who you are in Christ: your rights and your responsibilities.

Williams Ossai

Chapter One

Your Responsibility

Now he who plants and he who waters are one, and each one will receive his own reward according to his own labor.
— 1 Corinthians 3:8

Someone has defined responsibility as response to ability. Every man has a certain level of ability in him which he must put to use or exercise for productivity (output, yield) which is directly proportional to the ability. The more you exercise your ability, the better and stronger you become and the greater your yield or output.

Ability is generally expected to translate to enhanced productivity with application and discipline.

When God gives a man a responsibility, He first gives him ability. He (God) knows that the man has all it takes to succeed as expected when he puts the ability to effective use.

If that man fails to peak productivity, he is solely to blame, not because he does not have what it takes, but because he has failed to understand his specific role, and hence gets distracted.

The primary thing is to know what is expected of you, know your purpose, clarify the specific roles or tasks given. Our Lord fully understood His purpose. He declared it in His mission statement, *"I have come that they may have life, and that they may have it more abundantly"* (John 10:10).

Know your purpose, your responsibility. This is the very first step to productivity.

Let us go back to the very beginning in Genesis:

> *And the Lord God took the man and put him into the garden of Eden to* ***work it and keep it****. And* ***the Lord God commanded the man****, saying, you may freely eat of every tree in the garden, but you shall not eat of the tree of the knowledge of good and evil. For in the day that you eat of it you shall surely die (Genesis 2:15-17 MKJV).*

The Two-Fold Instruction

As seen in the text above, there are two major instructions that God gave to man when He created him. One was a command and the other, an occupation which involved working and keeping the garden of Eden.

Paying attention to the command and being obedient to it would make him successful in the garden and keep him in a healthy spiritual relationship with his creator. On the other hand, paying attention to and being diligent in the occupation would make him productive in the garden.

Closely looking at the two instructions, it becomes immediately clear that there is an immediate and dire consequence of breaking the command. '*And **the Lord God commanded the man**, saying, "Of every tree of the garden you may freely eat; but of the tree of the knowledge of good and evil you shall not eat, for in the day that you eat of it **you shall surely die**"*' (Genesis 2:16-17).

However, there was no direct and apparent consequence for failing to work and keep the garden.

Working the garden and keeping the garden were what was expected of the man to do having found himself in that environment, to fully mine all the rich goodness of the garden. This responsibility was for his good and general wellbeing.

These two distinct instructions were not mutually exclusive. The command kept the man in God while in the garden, while the occupation enabled him fully harness the rich blessings of the garden.

This begins to put in clear perspective why a lot of Christians who love God and enjoy a healthy relationship with Him seem to struggle in the area of productivity.

The two instructions are still very relevant today in keeping us rooted in God and excelling in life.

The Good Part, and the Other Part

In June 2009, I began a journey with the Lord. I dedicated myself to consistently seeking the face of the Lord, studying the word of God and meditating on it daily. As a result, my life has been enriched with life transforming revelations from God's word. The experience or the journey was indeed similar to the experience of Mary, the sister of Martha, who sat at the feet of Jesus and heard His word. Mary's choice compared to that of her sister Martha, who was busy "working" for Jesus, was commended by Jesus when He said that she *"has chosen that **good part** which shall not be taken away from her"* (Luke 10:41-42) – **the command part** (emphasis, mine).

The word "part", suggests that it (**command**/relationship building) was not complete in itself, there was another part – the occupation. Dear friend, the relevance of the command does not take away from the significance of the occupation.

In the course of my journey, I focused exclusively on the command part of the instruction and realized over time that I was not harnessing and enjoying the rich blessings of actually "working and keeping the garden." I still struggled in the areas of business, finance, and relationship.

Like Peter I cried out to God, "I have left all and followed You so why do I still struggle in these areas?"

> Then Peter began to say to Him, **"See, we have left all and followed You."** So Jesus answered and said, "Assuredly, I say to you, there is no one who has left house or brothers or sisters or father or mother or wife or children or lands, for My sake and the gospel's, who shall not **receive a hundredfold now in this time** — houses and brothers and sisters and mothers and children and lands, with persecutions — and in the age to come, eternal life (Mark 10:28-30).

One would immediately assume that, just because you are a Christian and spend time with the Master, everything will automatically become rosy because of the promise of the hundredfold blessing that Jesus referred to in the above text. So why is this hundredfold blessing not evident in our relationships and endeavors?

In spite of their commitment and service, the hundredfold prosperity is still not the personal testimony of many Christians. This becomes a crushing disappointment for many and they begin to question the faithfulness of God. I had found myself perplexed by my personal status quo in life, until the Lord illuminated the problem and gave me the strategies to succeed. He drew my attention to the significance of "the other part" - the occupation.

Occupation in this context does not refer to your being an engineer, banker, doctor, trader, etc. It is that specific occupation assigned to you by God whether it be spiritual and/or secular. It is in the doing of this specific work, that you will experience unending productivity and lasting success.

Personally, I have honed technical skills and gained experiences having worked and excelled in both the power and finance industry for over a decade. This was however not the specific, God-assigned occupation for me. He had to take me out of this comfort zone into the "garden" of writing where my hundredfold blessings are.

Peter had a similar experience. He had established himself as a successful fisherman with physical assets (boats and other fishing paraphernalia) and human assets working for and with him. His one-off uneventful outing (the day he encountered Jesus) was not enough to qualify him as a failure in fishing. God used that singular event to redirect his focus to a higher calling and occupation. Jesus said to Peter, *"Follow me and I will make you fishers of men"* (Matthew 4:19). This new occupation which was all new to Peter, required new training, new skill sets and discipleship. So, it does not matter how good you are in your work or occupation, you need to know for sure if that is really where God wants you to be. Dear child of God, you need to find your garden.

The Garden

> *The Lord God planted a garden eastward in Eden, and there He put the man whom He had formed (Genesis 2:8).*

From the above scripture, we see that God, very deliberately, placed Adam in the garden which was east of Eden. Note that this garden did not occupy all of Eden. It was in this very specific environment that Adam would enjoy God's grace for the work as well as the maximum load of God's blessings.

Every Christian, has a very specific garden planted by God with a sure guarantee of productivity through diligent work.

As I said earlier, I was "gainfully employed" and very well paid for many years but still had not located "my garden."

As a banker or a medical doctor, is banking or medicine your garden?

There is a story about a lady who had been working in an organization for many years. She was never fulfilled as she struggled on the job. Eventually, she lost the job. In a bid to find alternate sources of revenue, she picked again, her interest in dress making. Her first customers were her immediate circle of friends. Before long, she enjoyed great patronage from top government officials. The business grew, was established and became very profitable. During an interview, she said she loathed the seven years she had given her previous employment. She had finally found fulfillment.

Child of God, you will never know true fulfilment and prosperity till you locate the specific garden wherein lies your purpose.

God gave Paul a message exclusively for the gentiles; that was his garden. As long as he remained in that specific garden, he made tremendous headway regardless of the challenges. When he attempted to take the message to the Jews in Jerusalem, he was warned in a trance to depart Jerusalem immediately: *"Make haste and get out of Jerusalem quickly, for they will not receive your testimony concerning Me"* (Acts 22:18).

It was this same Jerusalem that Peter and the other disciples were assigned as their own garden. They were clearly commanded in Acts 1:4 *"not to depart from Jerusalem but wait for the promise of the Father."* The book of Acts catalogues the outstanding results these disciples got in Jerusalem after waiting.

Sadly, this was not the case for Paul, who in spite of the warning went to Jerusalem. There, he was arrested and imprisoned for two years. It is pertinent to note here that there was no supernatural intervention like the earthquake in Acts 16:25-40, or angelic liberation in Acts 12:5-10 on his behalf.

Also consider our perfect example Jesus. When it was time for Him to begin His public ministration, He had to relocate His dwelling place from Nazareth to Capernaum (Matthew 4:13). When He visited Nazareth again, He could not perform many miracles there. And it was not that He did not have the power to perform mighty works, but that location was not predestinated for the great miracles that followed Him in ministry. The people there did not receive Him with faith and it hindered His work.

> *Now He did not do many mighty works there because of their unbelief (Matthew 13:58).*

Take out time to seek God's face concerning your specific garden. For it is in that specific assignment that God's grace is released for your productivity. This is the second step towards productivity. Also, note that the location of your garden does not hinder or limit the spread and impact of your message and/or services.

Found the Garden. What Next?

God Himself has assigned the responsibility of increase to Himself, but for there to be increase, there must first be a planting or cultivation. God is not responsible for the cultivation. That responsibility is going to be borne a hundred percent by you. We are in a partnership with God. The bible describes us as coworkers (2 Corinthians 6:1). Each party has a clearly documented job description (tasks, roles, expectations). It is important to note here that our role of cultivation will always precede God's role of giving increase.

Having located the garden and understood the specific expectation or task, a lot of people are intimidated by the sheer scope of the work because they feel they do not have the ability or flair for it. A lot of times, as I said earlier, God would have to take you out of your comfort zone. Moses faced this dilemma when he gave the excuse that he had a speech defect (Exodus 4:10). In spite of that perceived weakness, God still used him to do the extraordinary because he acted in obedience.

Likewise, my core competence was not in writing. I could have spent time arguing with God to give me what I have natural aptitude, flair and training for. That would have wasted my time and kept me unproductive. I made a decision to step out in faith and put my trust in God's ability only. Hence this book and many others that are sure to bless lives.

I want to encourage you, no matter how unprepared you feel you are for the occupation, take that first step in obedience. Remember, the size of a seed is usually very small and insignificant compared to the harvest. Do not rationalize on ability or competence. Simply obey God and watch out for the extraordinary.

Chapter Two

Your Job Description

*And the Lord took the man and put
him into the garden of Eden to
work it and keep it.*
—Genesis 1:15 MKJV

When the Lord put man in the garden of Eden, He gave him a blank cheque in Genesis 2:16: *"Of every tree of the garden you may freely eat."* It is important to note that Adam did not plant the garden. He was ushered into a ready-made environment of blessings and goodness. However, the precursor to this delightful experience was in the fifteenth verse of the same chapter, where God gave Adam his job description to cultivate, work, dress, keep.

If Adam neglected this responsibility, no matter how healthy his relationship with God was, he would not have the vital experience of enjoying the rich blessings of the garden.

The Lord God indeed had created everything before man came but Genesis 2:5 tells us that there was no shrub or plant of the field yet in the earth and no herb of the field had yet sprouted. All these things had been spoken forth into existence but had yet still remained in its "potential state" *"...for there was no man to cultivate the ground."*

The above text underscores the significance of the man's role or responsibility to work. God has His own responsibility to cause it to rain on the earth causing increase, but the cultivation is the responsibility of man.

The man is expected to work and keep the garden. These two words may appear similar and interchangeable but they are not, as we will explain.

Work It

There are two facets of the work that God assigns to man:

1. Secular work
2. Ministry work

For some, their occupation may involve the two scopes of work in varying degrees, while for others the appointment may be a hundred percent ministry or a hundred percent secular. From the word of God, we see that Peter had a fulltime responsibility in ministry while Paul did both secular and ministry work (1 Thessalonians 2:9, 2 Thessalonians 3:7-9).

If your mission field falls a hundred percent within the orbit of secular work, God will still expect you to use this environment for His glory. Example, a fulltime medical doctor, whilst providing medical care and attention for his/her patients is expected, alongside, to give the word of life that will grow the faith of the said patient for the ultimate victory in that situation

Every work assigned to man by God, whether secular or ministry, becomes a potential means to provide for himself as well as others (1 Corinthians 9:13, Ephesians 4:28).

The importance of getting it right with the kind of work you do cannot be overemphasized. There is a direct correlation between the work you do and the type of life you live. If the job is not right, life would very likely be characterized by struggle, unfulfillment, lack and despair.

The work you do is an embodiment as well as an expression of who you are: an expression of your ability, your intellect, time, strength and sweat. In the wrong occupation, you do not give full expression to who/what God has made you and what He has blessed you with. If you continue in this state, it leads to atrophy or waste of God-given gifts/talents.

In Genesis 3:17-19, when Adam was taken away from the garden, where he enjoyed fellowship with God and was expected to give full expression to who he was in God, he began to die and was disconnected from the opportunity of eating from the tree of life.

Our relationship with God and the type of work we do determine the quality of life we live; it determines whether we are really living, struggling or sadly dying.

A lot of people today are miserable because they are in the wrong occupation and therefore cannot freely dispense all they have been blessed with.

Jesus said, *"My food is to do the will of Him who sent Me, and to finish His work"* (John 4:34). "Finish" in the text describes a state of fulfilment and completion. Jesus was able to attain this state because He was actively doing the will of the Father. The question is, dear child of God, in your current work or occupation, are you doing the will of God?

Keeping the Right Attitude at Work

If you have taken delivery of your specific job description and you have started the work, well done! But do not be misled to think that you will not experience challenges on your journey. It is easy to maintain an excellent upbeat attitude when things are going well. It is even more important to maintain the right attitude when you face challenges.

Think about it! As perfect and beautiful as the garden of Eden was, there was a serpent and he brought about doubts, fear and compromise.

Joseph was given his job description in a dream. He was going to be a great leader over his people. However, the joy and excitement of that dream very quickly metamorphosed into a journey of betrayal, pain, false accusation, loss of dignity, independence, etc. Through every scene of Joseph's journey, he kept up an attitude of excellence and integrity. On account of his integrity, Joseph was falsely accused and thrown into prison, but even in that situation, he kept on serving God by interpreting dreams in prison (Genesis 40:8-9). He could have chosen to question or accuse God for His "seeming unfaithfulness", and wallow in self-pity which could have cost him the actualization of his dreams.

It was the love of Joseph for God and honor towards God in his service that announced him and made him prime minister in Egypt. If Joseph had chosen to "outsmart" God or cut corners on his journey, though he may have enjoyed relative comfort in Potiphar's house, his work and probably his life would have been truncated.

Dear child of God, stay on course, stay true to the work at hand knowing that when you pass through the waters God has promised, you will not be overwhelmed (Isaiah 43:2). Be confident that with your right attitude, it can only end in testimony.

Timing in Work

God is a God of time and season, and has allotted time for every activity under heaven.

> *To everything there is a season, a time for every purpose under heaven: (Ecclesiastes 3:1).*

When God gives you a task, you are not at liberty to execute it when you will. He will always give you a time period for execution. And you have to respect His timeline to achieve the expected result.

Even the birth of Jesus was timed. If Jesus had not come at the time He did, Mary probably would not have been the mother. He probably would not have met the people that He worked with, like Peter, James, John, etc. His audience (the people He ministered to), would have been different. Also, the circumstances of His crucifixion and death would have been altered. Imagine if Jesus was born in our time, legal issues on the death penalty would have prevented Him from being crucified the way He was. The work of Jesus finished perfectly majorly because of a perfect alignment with God's timing.

Jesus instructed the disciples to wait in Jerusalem (physically present in Jerusalem to be empowered by the Holy Ghost). Their obedience led to the outpouring of the Holy Ghost upon them. This event of the outpouring, coincided with the event of the Pentecost. The bible records that a large number of people from *"every nation under heaven"* who were present for the event of the Pentecost were ministered to by the disciples who had just received the baptism of the Holy Ghost (Acts 2:5-12). In verse 41, the bible records that about three thousand people who heard Peter speak, accepted his message and were baptized. This birthed the church and began the spread of Christianity.

Imagine, if Peter and his friends had gone each to his own way, they would have missed a major season of their ministry and the great harvest of souls and blessings that followed.

Dear child of God, delay in obedience is indeed disobedience.

Yet another example in obedience in timing was Philip, who because of his obedience, met a eunuch from Ethiopia in transit. If he had delayed, he would never have met the eunuch again and probably the eunuch may have missed the opportunity of ever hearing the message and getting baptized (Acts 8:26-38).

When God demands obedience from you, He has already gone ahead to orchestrate human and material resources, opportunities, situations and circumstances for His glory. Your inability to be available at the right time could throw God's plan out of order.

Timing is of essence, whether in secular or ministry activity, and requires integrity, discipline and strength of character.

> *Look carefully then how you walk! Live purposefully and worthily and accurately, not as the unwise and witless, but as wise (sensible, intelligent people), making the very most of the time [buying up each opportunity], because the days are evil (Ephesians 5:15-16 AMP).*

Chapter Three

Secular Work

> *The Lord your God will make you abound **in all the work of your hand,** in the fruit of your body, in the increase of your livestock, and in the produce of your land for good. For the Lord will again rejoice over you for good as He rejoiced over your fathers.*
> — Deuteronomy 30:10

In the pursuit of goals in a secular scope of work, people often make the mistake of drowning out spiritual goals and priorities. You must understand very clearly, that you are first a Christian before you are a doctor, engineer, banker or trader. If you are a doctor, you are not a doctor practicing Christianity, but you are a Christian practicing medicine. The ability to see your secular job as God assigned and not just what you have as a result of a formal education, will give you clarity of purpose in the work.

So, the first point of note is that your secular work is ultimately for the glory of God.

The fact that God is involved in your secular work would demand a high level of competence, skill, ability, diligence, and professionalism on the job. Unlike your coworker who is a non-Christian, you are answerable not only to your bosses but also to God.

> *Bondservants, be obedient to those who are your masters according to the flesh, with fear and trembling, in sincerity of heart, as to Christ;* ***not with eyeservice, as men-pleasers, but as bondservants of Christ, doing the will of God from the heart*** *(Ephesians 6:5-6).*

From the above text, it is very clear that as long as you are doing that God-assigned task or work, no matter who happens to be giving the orders, you are really serving God in that secular job. Keeping that in mind, we would have to hold ourselves up to a higher degree of accountability. Therefore, we must be seen to be skilled, diligent, competent, professional and productive.

In your current field of work, can you sincerely carry out a self-appraisal of yourself on the job and be found satisfactory on all performance indices? Remember, to be able to effectively preach Christ in that secular field of work, you must first be above reproach in performing your job description.

Dear child of God, it may interest you to note that God is interested in when you resume at work, how you deal with your clientele, your deliverables and of course, your turnaround time on assigned duties. You may ask, why would God be bothered about such trivialities? These so called "trivialities" actually promote an enabling environment for the message of the kingdom.

Be Exemplary

Let us take a look at the young man Daniel. He was made a commissioner under King Darius and distinguished himself among the other commissioners. His colleagues tried to find a reason to bring a complaint against him concerning the administration of the kingdom; but they could find no reason for an accusation or evidence of corruption because he was faithful (a man of high moral character and personal integrity), and no negligence or corruption (of any kind) was found in him. These men said, *"We shall not find any charge against this Daniel unless we find it against him concerning the law of his God"* (Daniel 6:5).

Dear child of God, can you boast of a glowing testimonial from your colleagues, bosses, or clients?

Apply yourself, hone your skills pertinent to your job or work through trainings, further studies, and reading wide.

All these will have a positive impact not only on your productivity at work but also enhance your effectiveness in ministry.

Life is all about continuous improvement. Even Jesus **"*increased in wisdom and stature,* and *in favor with God and men"* (Luke 2:52). These exacting expectations also hold for secular workers who also run churches or fellowships. Paul was a full-time minister who occasionally engaged in the secular work of tent building. At such times, the secular work served as an example to the churches in discipline, hard work, and diligence (2 Thessalonians 3:7-9).

So, for you who are involved in the two facets of work, you should, through your secular work offer yourselves as a model or example for others to follow. God expects you to be effective and productive in the discharge of both your secular and ministry work. In 1 Thessalonians 2:9, Paul stated that they worked night and day practicing their trade... while they proclaimed the gospel. So, we can clearly see that they were diligent and effective in both ministry and tent building.

The Waiting Room

Some Christians have found themselves in situations whereby they know for sure that their current positions (work) is not their God-assigned task but are actually instructed to wait patiently awaiting further instructions. Example, you may be a medical doctor who having sought the face of the Lord, has become aware of a divine nudge/pull to a different scope of work as assigned by God, but is being prevented by God from leaving the current practice of medicine.

God is not an author of confusion. Such situations serve as a training period or preparatory ground for effectiveness in that "garden" (next level or scope of work).

The young man David was anointed by the prophet Samuel as king over Israel. However, Saul was still reigning as king in Israel at the time. David knew that the oil was speaking of a time in the future. The period of time that followed, served as training for David. It was not a very pleasant time for him. David's training period was rife with life threatening challenges, but in that time, he developed new skills set, developed strength of character and God equipped him with human and material resources for the time when he would be crowned king.

Dear child of God, if you have found yourself in a similar training period or waiting time, do not give yourself to murmuring or self-pity. Seize the moment, maximize the time. You will realize that when God eventually says "go", you will be richly equipped, and abundantly furnished for the next level of operation.

Very often, there is a strong temptation to step out of the waiting room prematurely. This is tantamount to failure. Sometimes, God may send you a "Saul" for the training. That Saul may be a very difficult boss or even senior pastor that makes the waiting almost unbearable for you. A lot of young pastors, because of this type of training, have prematurely broken away from ministries, churches or fellowships.

Because the timing was not right, they ended up struggling and unproductive even in their God-assigned tasks. Child of God, be wise. Believe me, no time is wasted if you are patient and apply yourself wisely.

> *Now no chastening seems to be joyful for the present, but painful; nevertheless, afterward it yields the peaceable fruit of*

righteousness to those who have been trained by it (Hebrews 12:11).

Operating by a Different Set of Rules

This topic does not in any way promote insubordination or disregard of authority. Remember, we said earlier that first and foremost, you are a Christian who is involved in that secular work or task. The results you get are very important to God. In any given industry or business, there are risks that are commonly faced by operators or key players in that business or industry. These risks, to a very large extent may negatively impact on output/productivity.

Dear child of God, always remember, that even in your secular work, there *is* a God factor. If you struggle on the job, struggle in your output, in the area of productivity, you will also struggle to preach Christ. God is an extraordinary strategist and will give you practical wisdom to mitigate against environmental risks and challenges thereby prospering your business.

In Acts 19:8-10, we are told that Paul went into the Synagogue and spoke boldly for three months, reasoning and persuading, concerning the things of the kingdom of God. His message however was not received. Instead of throwing up his hands in despair or pointing accusing fingers at God, he looked to God and God gave him a strategy. He took some disciples to the school of Tyrannus and there reasoned with them daily. He did this for two years and as a result, everyone who dwelt in Asia heard the message both Jews and Greek. That God-given strategy guaranteed a greater harvest.

Let us look at another great individual who operated by a different set of rules. Daniel again, this time under King Nebuchadnezzar, faced a challenge in the course of his work that threatened not only his office but his life as well. The bible registers in Daniel 2:1-22, that the king had a dream that perplexed him to the extent of insomnia. He summoned all his magicians, astrologers and wisemen to interpret the dream for him. They were unable to do so saying that there was no man on earth able to do the job. The king, in his rage, ordered the destruction of all the serving officers in these different capacities (including Daniel). Daniel sought God's help and the mystery was revealed to him.

Verse 22 of the same chapter says, *"He (God)reveals deep and secret things; He knows what is in the darkness, and light dwells with Him."*

God understands the challenges you face at work more than you ever can and not only is the solution or answer with Him but He will reveal them to you. Consequently, you are not expected to struggle or suffer as others.

Psalm 1:3 describes you as that tree that is *"planted by the rivers of water, that brings forth its fruit in its season."* Note that the word "river" is in plural. God Himself will give you multiple ideas, strategies, wisdom that is uncommon in that specific field. He will also furnish you with grace to succeed even when others struggle. Take time to understand the mind of God concerning your business. You are not ordinary, even in your secular work. You carry the presence of God and therefore should operate by a different set of rules.

When you are aware that God is involved in your business or career and avail yourself of His wisdom and grace, you immediately begin to operate from a vantage position.

Whatever secular job you are involved in, you are providing a service. God will always give you creative ideas on how to do better and stay ahead of competition. For example, there is this young man who roasts "bole" (plantain) and fish which is a staple in Rivers state, Nigeria. The young man has brought innovation, art and style to this business by introducing assorted vegetables to the meal as well as serving the meals in takeaway packs. He has gone a notch higher still, by providing delivery services and on-site services for parties and events. Consequently, in spite of the fact that he has charged a premium for all of these extras, patronage has increased and he has had to employ staff to enable him meet demand.

Don't ever be satisfied with the status quo. Challenge the status quo. The Spirit of God is dynamic and if you let Him, He will teach you how to make profit.

> *And you shall remember the Lord your God, for it is He who gives you power to get wealth, that He may establish His covenant which He swore to your fathers, as it is this day (Deuteronomy 8:18).*

Necessity – the Mother of Invention

Every human being is loaded with a lot of potential. Some are identified earlier and groomed to full potential and others are birthed under immense pressure, when faced with challenges. Indeed, necessity is the mother of invention.

For Adam and Eve, the creative ability to make clothes or covering was not expressed until they had fallen and realized they were naked and needed to be covered (Genesis 3:7). Where ever you find yourself, always think outside the box. Have a different mindset towards problems, difficulties and challenges. Don't join the world to gripe about life's challenges or difficulties.

Every challenge or difficulty is an opportunity to birth potential to meet a need. And every solution proffered translates to revenue or income. We have needs in the areas of housing, transportation, power, communication, recreation, education, information, feeding, industrialization, security, health, physical fitness, entertainment, leadership, etc. You have something on the inside that if allowed full expression, can solve complex problems in any one of the areas of need.

Go ahead! Develop yourself and be the solution that men seek.

> *For the earnest expectation of the creation eagerly waits for the revealing of the sons of God (Romans 8:19).*

Enjoying Multiple Streams of Income

The Holy Spirit also enables you to be multidimensional so you can, for example, be a medical doctor meeting other needs outside the medical field, and enjoy multiple streams of revenue as a result.

> *Put your investments in several places — many places even — because you never know what kind of bad luck you are going to have in this world (Ecclesiastes 11:2 GNT).*

Note that there is always a "buyer" for every problem solved or need met.

Remember the Lord Thy God

This topic is an extract from the Lord's command in Deuteronomy 8:18. Why would God caution His people to remember Him? Because God's people then and even today are falling into the danger of being distracted in their work for God.

The bible says in Matthew 5:16, *"Let your light so shine before men, that they may see your good works and glorify your Father in heaven."* God does not just expect you to shine in your secular field of work. The degree or extent of shining is important, because it is only a certain degree of shining that will bring forth a certain result. A lot of people get so overwhelmed and distracted by the demands of the job that in the end they make very little or no impact on the lives of the people the Lord brings to them daily.

Dear child of God, you need to understand fully that providing the service you do is not an end itself but merely a means to an end. Do not think for a moment that you happen on the people you meet daily by chance. They have been deliberately brought your way by God for a much higher purpose than just giving a service.

In the garden of Eden, the bible records that it was God Himself who brought the living creatures to Adam to see what he will name them (Genesis 2:19). So likewise, it is God Himself who brings the patients to the doctors, the customers to the traders, and clients to the bankers to see what you will do with them beyond giving them professional service. A lot of them come so dejected, oppressed, broken, abused, and leave exactly the same way, with no change in name, identity or status quo.

Remember the Lord thy God!

Remember your higher calling in Christ!

Chapter Four

Ministry Work

*Of which I became a minister
according to the gift of the grace of
God given to me by the effective
working of His power.*
—Ephesians 3:7

Ministry work is similar to secular work but takes on a slightly different trajectory. While secular work depends majorly on skill, competence or experience for the task, ministry work is effected through a specific call from God as well as spiritual gift(s) to make you effective in that call. It is important to note from the very beginning that irrespective of your mission field, every Christian has been given the ministry of reconciliation (2 Corinthians 5:18-19). Being involved in ministry work requires a greater investment of your time in praying, teaching, preaching and other related activities.

In ministry, it is important to know your area of specialization (apostle, prophet, evangelist, pastor and teacher). For when you function in that God assigned area, you become effective in the work of ministry (Ephesians 4:11-12).

All the avenues for ministry listed above require an effective means of communication, of which, the primary means of communication is your lifestyle.

Lifestyle

2 Corinthians 3:3 states clearly that, *"You are an epistle of Christ."* The second verse states that, *"You are read by everyone."* Not just your family or members of your ministry but by everyone.

Dear child of God, having been read by men, perceptions are automatically formed. If these perceptions go unchecked, mindsets are established which can ultimately affect the way people receive your message. To grow in ministry, it is important to carry out a routine self-appraisal thereby soliciting feedback.

The Lord Jesus asked His disciples, *"Who do men say that I am?"* (Mark 8:27). It was important for Him to know the perception of men. Interestingly, the responses were varied and not unanimous. Who do your brethren, family, coworkers, business partners, say you are? If the people are having difficulty accepting you, then they will have difficulty accepting your message because you cannot be separated from the message you preach.

It is not about living your life for the approval of men but to determine the impact of your person and message on the people and steer yourself back on course if you have strayed off.

> *Do you see a man wise in his own eyes?*
> *There is more hope for a fool than for him*
> *(Proverbs 26:12).*

Learn to solicit feedback. It is important in ministry. Also, be open minded about feedback. Take the necessary information pertinent to your personal growth and growth in ministry. Work on this first and very important means of communicating your message. If you get this right, a major portion of your work is done.

> *Therefore let him who thinks he stands*
> *take heed lest he fall (1 Corinthians 10:12).*

Self-Development

2 Corinthians 4:7 records that, *"We have this treasure in earthen vessels, that the excellence of the power may be of God and not of us."* How can this treasure in the

earthen vessels be enjoyed by everyone? In other words, how can you effectively communicate this treasure to the world?

The purpose of communication is to convey your thoughts and ideas clearly and unambiguously. It is said to be effective when both the sender (the preacher) and the recipient understand the same information as a result of the communication. This is where self-development comes in because the ability to express or communicate the message is as important as the message itself. Jesus developed and showcased a certain style in His preaching. Very often, He used parables to communicate His message.

Dear child of God, have you developed a communication style?

In Ecclesiastes 12:9-10, it is evident that the preacher had the word of truth but he pondered and searched out and arranged many proverbs, he sought to find acceptable words to communicate the words of truth. In the CJB (Complete Jewish Bible) version, it says, *"Kohelet worked to develop an attractive writing style, in which he expressed the truth straightforwardly."*

Communication here does not imply the use of fine diction or correct tenses or phonetics. It is not about adopting *"enticing words of man's wisdom"* but by learning of the Spirit the right approach, words, style to effectively communicate the truth. An attractive communication style on its own is empty, void of power and impotent. Any professor, lecturer, or anyone who is well schooled can afford to speak well but preaching is spiritual. You have to align the truth you have with the God given style of communication and the power of the Holy Spirit so that your words would come forth with a demonstration of the Spirit and of power (1 Corinthians 2:4).

Let us take a look at our perfect example, the Lord Jesus Christ. *"All who heard Him were astonished at His understanding and answers"* (Luke 2:47). The astonishment of the people came from not only what Jesus had to say but how He said what He had to say.

Some ministers today struggle in the work not because they do not have the truth to preach but because they have not yet developed an effective method to minister the truth.

2 Timothy 2:24 says, *"And the servant of the Lord.... must be a skilled and suitable teacher"* (AMP).

Take time out to pray, study extensively, research, and develop yourself for enhanced effectiveness in ministry. It is sad but true that some people do not receive the word of truth, simply because of the style of delivery. The onus therefore lies with you, child of God, to work at self-development.

Growing in Grace

You are a minister of the gospel, no matter where you find yourself, whether in the secular field of work or in fulltime ministry work. In the two areas of operation, grace is cardinal to productivity. No matter how professional, diligent and efficient you are in the discharge of your duty, it is grace that guarantees the productivity or end result. You cannot take grace out of your ministry, career, or business. Pastor Chris Oyakhilome said, "Your effectiveness and productivity in any assignment would be to the extent of the grace granted you to function or carry out that assignment."

> *And God is able to make all grace (every favor and earthly blessing) come to you in abundance, so that you may always and under all circumstances and whatever the need be self-sufficient [possessing enough to require no aid or support and furnished in abundance for every good work and charitable donation] (2 Corinthians 9:8 AMP).*

From the above scripture we see that though skill and competence are both cardinal to productivity at work, it is grace that makes you excel at every good work.

In addition, for you to do more, the Lord will have to give you more grace (James 4:6a). That additional grace takes you to a higher level of productivity. Suddenly you discover that you are able to do hitherto what you could not do.

Whether in the secular field or in ministry work, it is very important that we remain in constant fellowship with the Lord as we serve Him. 2 Peter 3:18 says, *"But grow in the grace and knowledge of our Lord and savior Jesus Christ."* How do you grow in grace? Grace is increased as we know the Lord more through the ministry of the Spirit and the word.

You cannot be too busy "doing God's work" to have time for Him. Deliberately and consciously make out time to fellowship with the Lord and hear from Him for in so doing, you grow in grace. This is your sure guarantee to a fruitful and productive life.

The Reward of Labor

If God were to give you an opportunity to make a choice between a job in an oil producing company with a six-figure income monthly, and full-time ministry as a teacher of the word in a church or fellowship, what would you choose? Believe me, most people would go for the first option because it appears to offer a more "attractive", secure and consistent reward for labor. They would believe that the "employer" would always meet its contractual obligation to pay as and when due.

If a man-made organization could generate such confidence from its employees, how much more God who is the monarch of the universe as well as your employer? It is sad that a lot of Christians are not confident enough in God to meet His obligation to daily load us with benefits (Psalm 68:19).

I will ask you this, dear child of God, do you know that God is a rewarder, that no time or effort in the work of the Lord is wasted? If we can be just as confident in God as a paymaster, as we are in reputable man-made organizations, it will totally change our approach and attitude to the work.

> *Therefore, my dear brothers, stand firm. Let nothing move you. Always **give yourselves fully** to the work of the Lord, because **you know** that your labor in the Lord is not in vain (1 Corinthians 15:58 NIV)*

The scripture above admonishes us to *"stand firm and let nothing move you."* It suggests that circumstances will arise in an attempt to shake you: unpaid bills, family and work pressures etc. Stay on course, refuse to resign or be distracted.

Ministry Work

The verse ends thus: *"Give yourselves fully to the work of the Lord, because you know that your labor in the Lord is not in vain."* What are your work ethics in full time ministry? Are you passionate and diligent or are you lackluster and withdraw at the slightest hint of challenges or problems? If you know that your labor (time and effort) in the Lord is not wasted, it will keep you fully focused and committed to the work. God is faithful. He is a rewarder. He has a far more robust payment and compensation plan for you than any company or organization in the whole world. Just stay true to the task and give yourself **fully (passionately, wholeheartedly and consistently)** to the work of the Lord.

God is sovereign and rules in the affairs of men. It is not up to you, the employee, to determine the means of the reward.

The bible tells us in 1 Kings 17:1-16 of how God sustained Elijah when there was famine for three and half years. God used ravens (birds distinctly known for their stingy and selfish nature) to feed Elijah twice daily. Elijah did not have to go out, looking for the ravens. They brought sustenance to Elijah.

Likewise, God can sustain you in the most unlikely and astonishing way. He will cause unlikely men to give to you simply because you serve Him faithfully.

From the same scripture, we see that shortly after Elijah's encounter with the ravens, He was directed by

God to a widow to be sustained by her though she was down to only her last meal. However, Elijah's presence in the widow's life and home brought about continuous provision and sustenance for Elijah and the widow's household. In the same way, God can connect you to an organization, enterprise or ministry at the verge of collapse, but due to your presence, is miraculously turned around and made viable. Also, in sustaining the organization, enterprise or ministry, you are also being sustained materially.

A Note on Receiving

> *Now you Philippians know also that in the beginning of the gospel, when I departed from Macedonia, no church shared with me **concerning giving and receiving** but you only (Philippians 4:15).*

In the above text, Paul talked about giving and receiving. In Christendom today, a lot of emphasis is placed on giving to the exclusion of receiving. As a minister of the gospel, receiving is just as important as giving. In the course of service, do you receive every gift or seed? How do you receive?

Let us look at the story of Gehazi. In 2 Kings 5:16, God used the prophet Elisha to heal Naaman of leprosy. In deep appreciation, Naaman offered a gift to Elisha but Elisha declined the gift and dismissed Naaman. Gehazi, Elisha's servant, ran after Naaman, caught up with him, and using falsehood, obtained some gifts from Naaman.

Elisha's response to Gehazi in verse 26 is quite illuminating. He said, *"Is it a proper time to accept money and clothing, and olive, orchards, and vineyard and sheep and oxen and male and female servants?"* Elisha's question suggests that there was nothing wrong with receiving the gift but the timing was not right.

Also, today, in the matter of receiving, God will always direct you on the right time to receive and what to do with the gift received.

Please note, not all seeds or gifts, when received are for your direct benefit or enjoyment. It is important to be led of God on not only whether to receive the gift but also how to utilize the gift. For instance, someone may give you a seed of one hundred thousand Naira and you have a pressing need for that amount. In spite of your own personal needs, the Lord may instruct you to give that seed to another minister, or do something with it that may not immediately take care of, or address your own personal need.

We need to be totally reliant on the leading of the Holy Spirit in the area of receiving so that we do not walk in error.

There is a way that seems right unto a man but the end thereof is destruction (Proverbs 14:12).

Gehazi received wrongly and it brought about a premature end to his service. Carefully consider how you receive so that what you receive does not kill your ministry.

Dear child of God, let it be abundantly clear that receiving in ministry is not all about you.

Chapter Five

Keep It

*And the Lord God took the man and put him into the garden of Eden to work it and **keep it.***
—*Genesis 2:15 MKJV*

In the previous chapters, we have dwelt extensively on working the garden. Looking at our theme scripture above, it is immediately clear that Adam was given a mandate to not only work the garden but keep it as well. The two words appear very similar, work closely together but are very distinctive. The words "keep it" come from the Hebrew word "shamar" which means keep, watch, preserve.

Working the garden in isolation is not enough to keep the man productive. The mandate is not mutually exclusive. Adam was expected to ensure that he excelled at both working and keeping the garden, to keep him productive.

Let us look closely at the expectations of keeping the garden.

1. Keep: To Keep Clean and Tidy

God is a God of order. He instructed Gideon to build an altar in the *"proper arrangement"* (Judges 6:26). There are many more examples in God's word that show us that God endorses order. Paul said to the Corinthians' church, *"Let all things be done decently and in order"* (1 Corinthians 14:40).

No environment can thrive or be productive in chaos.

Even the human body needs to be in order for optimum functioning and good health. If any part of the body is out of order, it affects the functionality of that part and most likely another.

Dear child of God, what is the state of your garden (home, workshop, office, relationships)?

A clean, tidy, well ordered workplace and lifestyle are fundamental to your being productive. One may ask, does it really matter, what does being clean and tidy have to do with succeeding on the job?

Let me give you a clear example. There was a woman on my street who had a super market. Her shop was well stocked and the prices of goods affordable.

However, people were unwilling to buy from her because the shop was always untidy and had an offensive smell. She finally closed down the business because it wasn't self-sustaining.

A few months later, the shop space was taken over by another person, who interestingly, opened another supermarket selling the very same goods. This time, the shop was very well organized and kept very clean and tidy. The result? It became the go-to shop for consumables and household items and a very profitable enterprise.

Do remember, that you as a Christian, represent Christ in your specific environment. Your output, results, are definitely not your own doing (not by your might, nor by your power, Zechariah 4:6).

It is God at *"work in you both to will and to do of His good pleasure"* (Philippians 2:13). That *"good pleasure"* cannot be accomplished in a filthy and offensive environment.

To buttress this point, let us take a look at Deuteronomy 23:12-14. God instructed the Israelites to go out of their camp to relieve themselves and to dig the ground to bury and cover their refuse. He went on to clarify why this was very important. In verse 14, God said, *"For the Lord your God walks in the midst of your camp, to deliver you and give your enemies over to you;*

therefore your camp shall be holy, that He may see no unclean thing among you, and turn away from you."

From this scripture, we can see there is a direct correlation between the cleanliness/order of the Israelites' camp and the victories they enjoyed over their enemies.

Dear child of God, let us go back to the basics. How does your work environment present itself to the senses? What is the sight, smell and feel of the environment you work in? Do you take out time to sweep and dust your office, clean the windows, wash the blinds and make sure your convenience is clean and smells fresh? Are your files organized? Documents well kept? Is your desk tidy?

You may feel all these things do not matter and are negligible to productivity. It matters to God and it should to you. These high standards of living are not only expected in your work place but also in your home. Is your living room tidy and devoid of clutter? Are the children's toys, shoes and irrelevant items scattered everywhere? Do your rest rooms have necessary items like tissue, soap, water? Does your home smell fresh and welcoming, or stale and uninviting? If your answer to any of the questions is a definite "no", or has even the slightest hint of uncertainty, then there is a lot of work to be done.

Remember, God is a God of order, and order ultimately, positively impacts on productivity.

Dress to be addressed

Then Pharaoh sent and called Joseph, and they brought him quickly out of the dungeon; and he shaved, changed his clothing, and came to Pharaoh (Genesis 41:14).

Your appearance says a lot about who you are and generally affects the response and attitude of others towards you. Appearance here does not mean whether or not you are dressed in designer labels or trendy fashions and styles.

It is all about personal care and hygiene. It starts from your hair. Is your hair well washed and groomed regularly? Accumulation of dirt and buildup of sweat in the hair produces a very offensive odor, very often undetected by the person in question. Take time to wash and groom your hair regularly.

Smell is a major turn off for anyone. The finest of clothes and trendiest fashions can never disguise an offensive odor. Apart from your hair, also pay keen attention to your breath. As a minister of God, whether in secular work or ministry, God will always bring people within your sphere of contact. Many times, you may have to transact with people at very close range. Is your breath fresh or stale, offensive and a turn off?

Take time out to brush and floss your teeth at least twice a day. Invest in a mouth wash and mouth fresheners if need be. Also, eat healthy because what you eat affects the health and state of your teeth/mouth. In addition, drink lots of water regularly because water helps keep your mouth and breath fresh.

The same care given to the mouth, applies to the body. Please remember that your body is the temple of God and His Spirit lives inside of you (1 Corinthians 6:19-20).

To be effective in ministry, it is important to take proper care of your body by eating right, exercising and personal hygiene. If your body's functionality is impaired due to lack of care and personal hygiene, it could jeopardize the work of the Spirit here on earth. The Holy Spirit requires your body to do His work and touch the world through you. The onus, therefore is on you to take proper care of your body.

Body odors generally arise from lack of or inadequate personal hygiene. Bathing should not only be done in the mornings. After the day's activities and chores, there will be a buildup of sweat and dirt on your skin. It is advisable to take a bath before going to bed at night.

Apart from your body, your clothes require proper care and attention as well. Wash your clothes and foundation garments immediately after wearing them once. This applies for both women and men as well.

Clothes that can be worn more than once without washing, e.g. trousers, jeans, skirts, etc., should be aired or sunned once removed. Air your shoes regularly and clean them once they are taken off.

Finger nails and toe nails are not left out in your body care and general appearance. They ought to be kept clean, trimmed and well groomed.

Dear child God, as I mentioned earlier, the importance of smell cannot be overemphasized. Invest in a good deodorant, body spray or perfume. Your smell should not hinder God at work in you.

Proverbs 27:9 underscores the importance of smell – *"Ointment and perfume delight the heart."*

2. Watch: Provide Security

*Then the Lord God placed the man in the Garden of Eden to cultivate it and **guard it** (Genesis 2:15 GNT).*

We shall look at yet another aspect of keeping the garden, which is security.

Why was security important in the garden of Eden? God Himself was present. There were no threat of intruders or harm, so why the mandate to provide security? It is important to note here, that in that very perfect environment called Eden, the serpent was present. And because Adam and Eve were not vigilant, they were driven from Eden.

Prior to this, what security checks or measures did Adam put in place in the garden to mitigate the risks of the serpent having access to Eve? It was Adam's responsibility to keep watch against the devil and its cohorts. The bible says that, *"Our adversary the devil is like a roaring lion, seeking whom to devour"* (1 Peter 5:8). The devil is actively seeking till this very moment. He will carry his search into your home, office, business and ministry, with the intent *"to steal, and to kill, and to destroy"* (John 10:10).

Yes, it is very important to have security guards, security systems (CCTV, security lights, alarms, car tracker, and police contact in place). However, all these measures on their own cannot provide protection against the devil and his cohorts. Psalm 127:1b says, *"Unless the Lord guards the city, the watchman stays awake in vain."* Unless the Lord is actively involved in your security and the security of your home, business or work place, all other security is in vain.

Take time out to declare words over your life, your home, and work place. Acknowledge daily that your life and the things that you do are hid with Christ in God. When you do this, you recognize that your security is guaranteed in God alone. Having done this, also ensure, that you provide a reasonable form of security for the human and material resources in your garden.

Ensure documents, and all relevant business, financial or personal information are secured. Ensure all the information on your mobile devices, PCs, are well secured.

It is also wise to invest in CCTVs and alarms for the home, office and vehicles.

Adopt a safety-first approach in your home and work environment. Keep your home and work environment safe at all times. Pay attention to your gas cylinders, sockets in the home or office and fix any faulty socket, gas cylinders in your environment. Keep harmful appliances away from children. Always have a functional fire extinguisher in your home, office and vehicle.

Security intelligence

Ensure security checks on all your staff, whether domestic or official. A lot of crimes happen today through domestic staff.

It is important to pay attention to information that borders on security in your immediate environment, city or state at large. Keep yourself well informed via updates on your radio and TV stations, as well as other reliable information channels. It may save your life or the life of a loved one.

Paul found himself in a similar predicament in Acts 23:12, "...*some Jews banded together and took an oath that they would neither eat or drink till they had killed Paul,"* and the information got to Paul himself. He did not make light of the information he received. He raised alarm and security measures were put in place to avert the disaster. If he had failed to respond promptly to the information received, his life and wellbeing would have been gravely threatened.

Ephesians 6:13 says, *"Therefore take up the whole armor of God, that you may be able to withstand in the evil day, and having done all,* **to stand***."*

In providing security, God has a part to play and so do you.

Ties that bolster security

In keeping with reinforcing security, your physical environment matters. It is not wise to take up residence in a desolate environment, devoid of human presence and activity. Doing this would open you up to constant attacks from intruders, thieves and armed robbers. You will do well to scope the area you are prospecting before drawing your conclusions. How close is your nearest neighbor? Is there commercial activity in the area? What kind of people live around you? It is important to carry out these security checks before moving into an area, or you may inadvertently be moving into a den of thieves.

In addition, how is the relationship between you and your neighbors? Is it warm and cordial, or distant and aloof? It is important to cultivate a cordial relationship and enjoy ties with the people living around you. In the event that there is a threat of intrusion or a security breach, with a cordial relationship in place, it is easy for a neighbor to give you a warning call or signal.

Judges 18:27-28 describes the invasion of a quiet and secure city. The people were destroyed and the city burnt with fire because there was no deliverer. It was far from Sidon, and they had no ties with anyone. On the other hand, when Abraham's nephew, Lot, was captured, information got to Abraham swiftly, due to proximity, and because of proximity, Abraham was able to raise an army to rescue Lot (Genesis 14). It is important, not only to have neighbors, but to maintain cordial ties with the people around you. Dear child of God, these ties may one day save a life.

3. Preserve: Protect the Interest

*The Lord God took the man and placed him in the orchard in Eden to care for it and **to maintain it** (Genesis 2:15 NET).*

Every environment represents an interest. The interest of a school is teaching and education. The interest of a hospital is providing health care.

Whatever your environment, it is your responsibility to protect the essence of that environment. For example, in your home, you cannot cook in the bedroom and sleep in the kitchen. That is clearly an abuse of the environment.

Dear child of God, is the essence of your home/office protected? Are things kept in order and used appropriately?

Jesus was furious with some people, because they had, by their trading activities, tried to alter the essence or purpose of the temple. He said, *"My house shall be called the house of prayer, but you have made it the 'den of thieves'"* (Matthew 21:13).

Is your office or business place disorganized by domestic concerns?

There are offices that have been literally turned into dressing rooms, with several pairs of shoes or changes of clothing littered everywhere. In some business environments, you can find pots, plates, etc. scattered about.

It does not speak well of the business owner, when one walks into a business premises permeated with a strong smell of food. If you must eat in your office, ensure that the used utensils are packed away out of sight. The windows are opened and the room freshened with air freshener.

For some people, their vehicle becomes a mobile shop. This is okay but it is no excuse for an untidy car with "goods and business items" scattered all over the seats and floor. In such cases, all merchandise should be kept neatly in the boot. The interest of your vehicle must also be protected. Your vehicle is not your house, clear all change of clothing, extra shoes, water bottles out of the car and keep your vehicles clean, tidy and uncluttered.

Protecting the interest of the garden goes beyond protecting the essence of the environment. It also involves protecting the time allotted to your work or home life. Discipline and order are key. Time is a critical resource and must be judiciously spent and properly accounted for. Keep the hours allotted to business, strictly for your business. Keep the time allotted for family strictly for family. Strive to maintain a healthy work-life balance.

The bible says in Ecclesiastes 3:1, there is time for every activity under heaven. Effective time management is key to productivity. The bible admonishes us to *"make most of our time"* (Ephesians 5:16).

To ensure effective time management, plan your day. Learn to have a to do list daily, and prioritize your activities daily.

Getting a diary or small note book will enable you successfully schedule and plan your activities daily.

It is a personal practice for me which has helped me accomplish a lot on a daily basis. It also enables me routinely evaluate my achievements/outputs.

I recommend this practice as an effective tool in time management.

Chapter Six

Built by Design

*For You formed my inward parts;
You covered me in my mother's
womb. I will praise You, for I am
fearfully and wonderfully made;
marvellous are Your works, and
that my soul knows very well.*
—Psalm 139:13-14

There is deliberateness in all of creation. A perfect fusion of design and function. Let us take a close look at creation as we know it. All the fishes and aquatic organisms have specific organs or unique adaptations that enable them live successfully in water. If you take a fish, for example, out of its specific natural habitat (saltwater or freshwater), it will not survive more than a few minutes to hours because it is not designed for such habitat.

The very same pattern of deliberateness in creation applies to us humans. You may ask how? All human beings look alike and function in the same way. NO! You are the only one of your kind in the entire universe.

No one looks like you and no one can function like you. God specially designed you and everything about you – your strengths and even your weaknesses, the way you reason, your habits, disposition, temperaments, hobbies, mental acumen, personalities, everything about you is deliberate and unique to fulfilling a purpose. The question is, have you come to that point, where you acknowledge, embrace, cultivate and celebrate your uniqueness?

At this point in your life, can you say with full conviction, I know who I am, I know why I came, I understand my purpose?

We mentioned in chapter one that Jesus understood exactly why He came, and that knowledge guided Him, His relationships, His occupation, His habits, His locations, etc. He knew exactly who He was, Why He came and was so consumed by His purpose that He lived a successful life.

"I will praise You, for I am fearfully and wonderfully made". When you realize who you are in God and why you are here, it will give your life a meaning. You will live a life of purpose and your life will give God glory.

Many people of God today, not only have they not discovered the purpose for which they were born, but have completely veered off track, found themselves in wrong occupations, wrong locations, wrong relationships and even wrong marriages, leading empty and unfruitful lives.

When Zacchaeus met Christ, he was a successful tax collector albeit a known sinner. His life with all of its wrong turns was completely changed the day he met Christ. He gave to the poor and returned money to those he had by any means cheated. By so doing, he aligned himself to his divine design through his renewed work ethics; remembering the poor and not cheating. And Jesus said to him (Zacchaeus), *"Today salvation has come to this house, because he also is a son of Abraham"* (Luke 19:9).

His true identity was the son of Abraham who loved God and men, not one who neglected the poor and defrauded the innocent.

An adulteress, caught in the very act, was about to face a death sentence when she encountered Jesus. She was given a new life and purpose. The testimony of her change was to give hope to the hopeless and downtrodden in life. (John 8:1-12)

It does not even matter whether you are a Christian or not at the moment. Through this book, God is giving you an opportunity to have a life changing encounter, that will set you on the course that is predestinated for you so you can succeed in life.

Discovering Purpose

A lot of Christians, prior to embracing their design and purpose, have undergone series of formal and informal trainings in life, been shaped by a lot of direct and indirect influences, pressures and life's demands. A lot of people today, by default, are living another person's dream – parent's, mentor's, role model's, etc.

In the quest to succeed in life or attain some level of fulfilment, decisions are being made almost daily, that either align you with God's perfect plan and purpose for you, or throw you out completely.

The fact that you may actually be enjoying some level of success with the decisions made, does not alter God's specific plan for you. As I said earlier, I enjoyed success in my career path but when I embraced my specific design and purpose, God took me on a completely new and fulfilling journey of writing.

By human parameters, it is possible to be too young, too old, under qualified or over qualified for a certain job; but with God, whenever you say "yes"' to His leading and direction, is the right time to begin your journey of true success. Let nothing stop you from embarking on that journey.

Let us take Moses for example; he was raised prince of Egypt. In his forties, he embraced God's specific plan for his life. He came to terms with his design and purpose. He was wrong in his first execution and had to flee Egypt. However, his ministry did not start when he fled Egypt. He had to spend yet another 40 years in the wilderness undergoing training as a shepherd. He eventually returned to Egypt in his eighties, to fulfil God's purpose. Did Moses, having started so late in life, succeed in ministry? YES! He enjoyed forty years of mind-blowing triumphs, signs and wonders. Though he may have started "late", he made tremendous impact.

Imagine for a moment, that after long years of training, you have qualified as a specialist in the medical sciences for example. You have distinguished yourself in the medical field and earned the professional respect of your colleagues as well as the trust of your patients. At this point, God directs you on a totally different and unrelated career path, like running a daycare/creche on a fulltime basis.

Understandably, that kind of transition is never easy. The period would most likely be characterized by questions, analysis and arguments. A lot of Christians have arrived at this valley of indecision, not knowing how they can proceed on a journey they feel totally unprepared for.

Dear child of God, I too came to the point in life, where I asked a lot of questions because for me the transition was just as drastic. I finally realized that all I needed to do was say "yes" and when I did, everything came together for me. I can tell you, that from the very beginning of the journey, I have enjoyed peace and fulfilment in being in the center of God's plan and purpose for my life.

Just take that first step in faith. I guarantee you will not regret it. God is too faithful for you to fail.

> *But seek first the kingdom of God and His righteousness, and all these things shall be added to you (Matthew 6:33).*

Dear child of God, seek first your place, your value, your identity, your occupation and your purpose in the kingdom of God to enable you effectively expand the message of the kingdom and truly succeed in life.

Be Useful

> *Let him who stole steal no longer, but **rather let him labor, working with his hands what is good**, that he may have something to give him who has need (Ephesians 4:28).*

Paul had the audacity to say this to the church at Ephesus because he was self-reliant. God's grand plan for us all is to be fruitful, productive and self-sufficient, requiring no external aid or support (2 Corinthians 9:8).

Dear child of God, in your current position, are you truly self-sufficient, or do you rely on another for even the very basic requirements of life? You may say, I am forced to, because I am not working right now. You need to change the status quo right away because that status quo does not give God glory.

As a child of God, do well to remember that you are blessed to be a blessing. It is up to you to develop yourself; learn a skill, serve as an apprentice, start a trade, no matter how small. This segment seeks to address self-development, being useful to yourself and others. Your preoccupation at this point may not be finding God's perfect plan but to earn a living, be paid for providing a service.

Let us look at Paul. He had developed a skill set for tent making, which enabled him take care of his needs.

> *For you remember, brethren, our labor and toil; for laboring night and day, that we might not be a burden to any of you, we preached to you the gospel of God (1 Thessalonians 2:9).*

> *For you yourselves know how you ought to follow us, for we were not disorderly among you; nor did we eat anyone's bread free of charge, but worked with labor and toil night and day, that we might not be a burden to any of you, not because we do not have authority, but to make ourselves an example of how you should follow us (2 Thessalonians 3:7-9).*

Paul decided to fend for himself sometimes, and not depend on the churches so that the gospel would have an unhindered course in the lives of those who heard.

Note, Paul was not being paid in tent making simply because he was a respected apostle of Christ, he was being paid FOR his skill in tent making. His being an apostle could be an added advantage in enjoying increased patronage, because of his influence and integrity.

From Ephesians 4:28, we can always infer that there is always something good you can do to earn a living. **Find it, no matter how small, and grow from there.**

> *But we urge you, brothers and sisters, to do so more and more, to aspire to lead a quiet*

life, to attend to your own business, and to work with your hands, as we commanded you. In this way you will live a decent life before outsiders and not be in need (1 Thessalonians 4:10-12 NET).

The above scripture underscores the importance of working and being productive. I love the word "aspire", which means to seek. So, seek! Make attempts to be involved in a good work, to live a life that will enable the gospel have free course.

If you are idle right now, aspire to get out of that situation for your own self-respect. There is dignity in all good labor. Never find yourself pressured to cut corners in life. Contrary to popular opinion, the end does not always justify the means.

A faithful man will abound with blessings, but he who hastens to be rich will not go unpunished (Proverbs 28:20).

For the love of money is a root of all kinds of evil, for which some have strayed from the faith in their greediness, and pierced

> *themselves through with many sorrows (1 Timothy 6:10).*

As you engage yourself in that good work, and continue to seek after God earnestly, God will orchestrate your steps to the very center of His purpose for you.

> *The steps of a good man are ordered by the Lord, and He delights in his way (Psalm 37:23).*

As you do this:

- You will lead a quiet life
- You will attend to your own business
- You will work with your hands
- You will live a decent life before outsiders
- You will not be in need

Designed to Be Self Sufficient

Dear child of God, I want you to understand that God does not want His children to live in poverty. Jesus came, not only to deliver man from sin, but also from poverty.

> *For you know the grace of our Lord Jesus Christ, that though He was rich, yet for your sakes He became poor, that you through His poverty might become rich (2 Corinthians 8:9).*

I am sure you have heard this said, that the gospel is free but not cheap. This is so true. How will we effectively send the message of God's undying love to all of mankind, if we are not financially empowered to do so?

> *Again proclaim, saying, 'Thus says the Lord of hosts: "My cities shall again spread out through prosperity; The Lord will again comfort Zion, and will again choose Jerusalem"' (Zechariah 1:17).*

From the above scripture, we see that the kingdom of God spreads through prosperity. Whose prosperity? The government will not finance the gospel, neither will the private sector, politicians, or high net worth individuals. It is the prosperity of the children of God that is being referred to in that scripture. That is why necessity is laid on us, to be engaged in good work, because God will not bless idle hands.

Poverty is not just the absence of money, it is a mindset. Refuse to be poor for that is not your true design. When you accept poverty, you lose your right and privileges of prosperity in Christ, for prosperity is a part of the package of the full benefits of salvation. The Lord Jesus gave up His status and identity of prosperity so that we may gain it. That is your present right and privilege in Christ. First know it, then insist on it. Exercise your right of prosperity by refusing to be poor, no matter the circumstances. If you are not enjoying this particular benefit of salvation, you are entirely to blame. *For as a man thinks in his heart, so is he* (Proverbs 23:7).

> *He who tills his land will have plenty of bread, but he who follows frivolity will have poverty enough! (Proverbs 28:19)*

> *For even when we were with you, we commanded you this: If anyone will not work, neither shall he eat. For we hear that there are some who walk among you in a disorderly manner, not working at all, but are busybodies. Now those who are such we command and exhort through our Lord Jesus Christ that they work in quietness and*

eat their own bread (2 Thessalonians 3:10-12).

The rich man's wealth is his strong city; the destruction of the poor is their poverty (Proverbs 10:15).

Chapter Seven

Acquiring New Skills

> *As for these four young men, God gave them knowledge and skill in all literature and wisdom; and Daniel had understanding in all visions and dreams.*
> —Daniel 1:17

We all know the story of David, the diligent shepherd boy, who took care of his father's sheep. To meet the prerequisites to succeeding as a shepherd, he had to understand the sheep as well as the practice of sheepherding. Over and beyond knowing the best areas for grazing and watering, he also had to develop the ability to protect the sheep from predators (lions and bears).

This ability was found useful also, when he faced Goliath of Gath, the Philistine.

King Saul offered David his fighting attire and his sword to confront Goliath with, but he could not use them because he had no previous experience with the use of the armor, hence he opted for his tried and trusted sling.

> *David strapped on his sword over his fighting attire and tried to walk around, but he was not used to them. David said to Saul, "I can't walk in these things, **for I'm not used to them.**" So David removed them (1 Samuel 17:39 NET).*

In this particular confrontation, his skill with the sling sufficed in giving him and the Israelites total victory over Goliath and the Philistines. The strategy of the sling was effective in that battle because it was a one on one fight.

Very soon after, David was faced with a situation that demanded an entirely new skill set. It was still in the line of battle, but this time, his skill set with the sling would not suffice.

David was anointed king over Israel. As a king, he was expected to lead his army into battle. Such battles were not to be fought and won with slings. To be adequately prepared for the demands of kingship, he had to develop an entirely new skill set – using fighting attire and the sword.

Why was a new skill set required for David? He had enjoyed tremendous success with the sling, so why did he not depend on that skill for all subsequent battles?

The confrontation, for which the sling was effective, was quite unique in that time – a one on one confrontation. Fighting enemy nations was typically a free for all fight, where your dexterity with a sword was required. It was also very necessary in such fights to be fully equipped with armor so that you would not fall prey to an arrow shot from a distance or a sword at close range.

Being effective is about staying relevant in your specific task or duty. Staying relevant very often comes with updating or honing a particular set of acquired skills or developing an entirely new set of skills depending on where God leads you.

I had mentioned in chapter three that life is about continuous improvement. You are the object of that continuous improvement. Never come to a place in your life, job or ministry where you feel you have arrived. Always be hungry to outdo your past. This is where training and development is key. Take relevant courses, read/research extensively to understand new and better ways of getting the job done.

Even as a pastor, do not be satisfied just getting rhema from the word. Read extensively, get a mentor you can learn from regularly and yes, take a course in public speaking. When you spend time to improve yourself and prepare, the impact is stronger and lasts longer.

Note that regardless of the anointing upon David's life, he would not have survived one day in a free for all battle with the sling. For enhanced effectiveness, David improved himself by learning the relevant strategy for battle and also learning to collaborate with people (1 Samuel 22:2).

Nevertheless, regardless of the need for self-improvement to stay relevant, victory ultimately comes from God, for the battle is not unto the strong, neither is the race to the swift. David understood this, when he said in 1 Samuel 17:47, *"...the Lord does not save with sword and spear; for the battle is the Lord's, and He will give you into our hands."*

> *The horse is prepared for the day of battle, but deliverance is of the Lord (Proverbs 21:31).*

Relational Skills

To be effective in your work, you will always need to work with people to get the job done. Sadly, a lot of anointed Christians struggle in their results because they have not developed relational skills.

God has underscored the importance of collaboration severally in the bible, with these few examples;

1. Two are better than one, because they have a good reward for their labor (Ecclesiastes 4:9).
2. The Lord appointed seventy others also, and sent them two by two before His face into every city and place where He Himself was about to go (Luke 10:1).

From the above scriptures we see that you are more productive working together with people of like mind. Let us look at yet another example.

> *As they ministered to the Lord and fasted, the Holy Spirit said, "Now separate to Me Barnabas and Saul for the work to which I have called them." Then, having fasted and prayed, and laid hands on them, they sent them away (Acts 13:2-3).*

The Lord chose Saul and Barnabas to do a special work. This was a great gospel team constituted by the Holy Spirit Himself.

One would imagine that this anointed team would continue to work in unity as well as record outstanding results. Understandably, disagreements would arise, which would be resolved amicably with the wisdom of God.

Alas, this was not the case for Paul and Barnabas. A strong contention arose in the course of their work, when Barnabas wanted John called Mark to travel with them on a particular mission and Paul insisted on not taking him. This disagreement, caused the separation of this divinely constituted team and short-circuited the great plan God had for them as a team.

Interestingly, also, nothing was ever heard again of Barnabas. Sad, but true what dissensions and disagreements can do to God's plan in your life.

Dear child of God, how is your relationship with your spouse, neighbors, colleagues, bosses? You cannot live in isolation.

God has sent people to you at any given point in your life to enhance your productivity. Your ability to live and work well with them is important to your succeeding in life and ministry.

Amos 3:3 asked a pertinent question, *"Can two work together, unless they are agreed?"*

This scripture does not suggest in any way that there will never be disagreements with the people you live and work with. It teaches that with the wisdom of

God, you are able to develop relational skills to maturely confront and handle disagreements in love.

Maybe Paul and Barnabas needed to develop relational skills. They could have approached the matter differently, resolved their issues amicably and continued in the work for which they were divinely commissioned.

Dear child of God, this is not something to take lightly. We have seen inability to agree, end marriages, relationships, work, and ministry. They ended, not because God did not institute them, but because the parties involved could not live or walk in unity.

The bible admonishes us in Romans 12:18 to the best of your ability, live peaceably with all men (more so with those you have to live and work with). (Emphasis, mine).

David said to Saul, *'"I can't walk in these things, **for I'm not used to them**." So David removed them.'*

Start today! Build/strengthen your relational skills. Learn to live in peace, even with the most difficult people. By so doing, you are respecting God's sovereign judgment for the people He sends to you as well as the objective for the collaboration.

Strength in Unity

There is nothing we cannot achieve or accomplish in life when working in unity. In Genesis 11:6, we understand that the whole earth was of one language, and proceeded to build a tower. The bible describes that they were one. Of them, God said in Genesis 11:6, *"Now nothing they have imagined they can do will be impossible for them"* (AMP).

Even God could not stop their work, because they were one. To stop work on the building, even God had to confuse their language. No devil can effectively stand against a people united. This is key in being happy and productive, whether in marriage, work or ministry. However, use your unity for God's glory.

> *And they said, "Come, let us build ourselves a city, and a tower whose top is in the heavens; let us make a name for ourselves, lest we be scattered abroad over the face of the whole earth" (Genesis 11:4).*

Though the people were truly united, they did not respect God's objective for making them united. They were supposed to leverage on their unity to form a **movement**, and spread to *"fill the earth and subdue it"* as God instructed in Genesis 1:28. Instead, they became wise in their eyes, and decided to employ their unity, by physically dwelling together in one location (a plain in the land of Shinar). There, they commenced in building a **monument** to make a name for themselves. God was displeased and disbanded them. Because of their cunning, God used chaos and confusion, to scatter the people all over the earth.

We see a similar scenario in the book of Acts, the believers were united by the Holy Spirit to spread the gospel beyond Jerusalem: to Judea, Samaria and to the ends of the earth (Acts 1:8) as they were commissioned. Instead they all remained in Jerusalem. However, persecution came and they got scattered. As a result, the gospel also spread along with them.

Use your relationships at work, in ministry and even your family to expand the course of the kingdom as God directs you. Never use your relationships to pursue a different agenda due to personal aspirations and gain.

Remember, there is a purpose for every God-instituted relationship/partnership. Pursue that purpose with unity.

Relational skills in marriage

You may wonder why we must veer into marriage. You may ponder the relevance of marriage to "working and keeping the garden." It is essential for us to take this very necessary detour into building/reinforcing relational skills in marriage. If you do not get it right in your marriage, it would negatively impact on every other area in life.

Dear child of God, I ask again, "How is your relationship with your spouse?" You cannot be said to be a success, whether in ministry or in secular work if you are not succeeding in your marriage.

Relational skills, nurtured by the word of God, is a *very* critical ingredient in the success of any marriage.

1 Peter 3:7 urges husbands to dwell (live) with their wives *"according to knowledge."* The amplified version gives us a deeper understanding – *"In the same way you married men should live considerately with [your wives],* **with an intelligent recognition [of the marriage relation]***."*

Note the words *"intelligent recognition."* Synonyms of the word intelligent include intellectual, scholarly, sensible, rational, logical and perceptive. Marriage is not all about spirituality (things about the spirit). Success in marriage is in part spiritual and in part, intellectual (relating to the mind or intellect).

Intelligence in that scripture, does not mean your intelligence as a lawyer, or teacher, or doctor; but an intelligence that comes from developing the required relational skills to live with your wife.

Do you have an intelligent recognition of your marriage relationship? How well do you understand your wife, her needs, her weaknesses, her moods and all the things and nuances that make her the unique woman she is? If you do not have an intelligent recognition of your wife and of your role as a husband, your home will not experience bliss, no matter how long you pray and how regularly you fast.

Take time to invest in your spouse. Develop a work-life balance. Your spouse needs as much attention as your work and ministry. Do not let her suffer emotionally, financially, mentally or physically because you are "busy" trying to succeed in life.

In marriage, you will need to develop yourself and adopt a strategy that works. Improve yourself regularly. Read good books/articles on marriage and romance, ask her open-ended questions on the best ways to keep her happy and satisfied. Solicit feedback on strategies to keep and improve on, as well as others to immediately discard. Remember, I said previously in chapter four that even Jesus solicited feedback from His disciples.

The institution of marriage is given top priority by God Himself. God likens marriage to the relationship of Christ and the Church. It is only in marriage that men are given a charge to imitate Christ even unto death.

> *Husbands, love your wives, just as Christ also loved the church and gave Himself for her (Ephesians 5:25).*

God respects the marriage relationship over and beyond blood ties. And if God would make demands on a man concerning his brother, like He asked Cain concerning Abel (Genesis 4:9), He would do even more for a man concerning his wife. Dear brothers, do not ever take your wives or your marriages for granted because this is your responsibility to God.

Let us borrow a leaf from how Jesus related with the disciples. Jesus knew each and every one of them intimately. He understood their individual strengths and struggles. Remember that He knew and pre-informed Peter that he (Peter) would deny Him three times.

In addition, Jesus knew, even before Judas himself, that Judas would betray Him. In the two scenarios, Jesus did not castigate, berate, accuse or blame the two disciples but still responded to them in love.

The bible says that Jesus, *"Had no need that anyone should testify of man, for He knew what was in man"* (John 2:25).

Jesus did not need anyone to inform him about His disciples. He knew them individually, and knew how to work with them all.

The wives are not left out of fulfilling their obligations in marriage. The wife is expected to approach her responsibilities with the same sense of gravity.

Ephesians 5:24 – But as the church is subject to Christ, so also wives should be subject to their husbands in everything (respecting both their position as protector and their responsibility to God as head of the house)

> *And let the wife see that she respects and reverences her husband [that she notices him, regards him, honors him, prefers him, venerates, and esteems him; and that she defers to him, praises him, and loves and admires him exceedingly] (Ephesians 5:33b AMP).*

These two scriptures, to a large extent, clearly, expressly and unambiguously capture the wife's responsibility to her husband.

I particularly like the phrase in verse 33, *"let the wife see that."* Against all odds, whether convenient or not, no matter how you may feel, ensure you do not fail. The bible in Ephesians 5:22 describes the wife's submission as service to the Lord.

Unfortunately, many women, due to circumstances, have transferred this devotion to their husbands to the children, business or career. Consequently, the husband is not delighted in, not preferred and treasured or made priority.

Don't reverse the order. No matter the pressures you may go through as a woman, trust God's word. Serve God in your submission and He will fight for you and bring calm, beauty and order to your life and home.

Developing Your Intelligence

First of all, you are a spirit being, but to effectively communicate, live and work in the physical world, God gives you intelligence. Intelligence here refers to your ingenuity as a farmer, doctor, lawyer, technocrat, engineer, trader, soldier, entrepreneur or any other occupation, through which you can express leadership or dominance.

Do not assume that growing spiritually should reduce your intelligence. As a spiritual being, recognize that your intelligence is given by God and use this intelligence appropriately. A successful blend of spirituality and intelligence yields productivity in any given area.

> *...But a nation will be strong and endure when it has intelligent, sensible leaders (Proverbs 28:2 GNT).*

Acquiring New Skills

Dear child of God, celebrate your spirituality as well as your intelligence. Joseph did just that when he not only interpreted Pharaoh's dream, but gave actionable plans for survival during the seven years of famine.

Joseph did not only rely on his dream interpreting ability to store food for seven years and then sell them in time of famine. The task required intelligence (applied wisdom – ability to implement it).

> *Now therefore, let Pharaoh select a **discerning and wise man**, and set him over the land of Egypt (Genesis 41:33).*

This recommendation was given by Joseph himself in his submission to Pharaoh. He knew that it would take, not only a discerning (spiritual) man, but also a wise (sensible) man to interpret and implement the right strategy for survival in Egypt.

Dear child of God, spend time growing in the knowledge of God's word. Also build on your intellectual capacity, and unleash both your spiritual and intellectual prowess in your work and ministry.

Like Joseph, God could divinely orchestrate events and give you a great job opportunity. However, your performance on the job will be based to a large extent on your intellectual competence and relevant skills.

Practice Maturity

But when Jesus saw it, He was greatly displeased and said to them, "Let the little children come to Me, and do not forbid them; for of such is the kingdom of God" (Mark 10:14).

The scripture above encourages us to be childlike in keeping God's command. As a child would - love easily, forgive easily, be teachable, be loveable, do not hold grudges or malice, etc. However, handling the issues of life – business, career, marriage, family and ministry requires maturity as men. Why do I say maturity as men? Because you will be required to take responsibility, and suffer consequences as a mature man.

*Brethren, do not be children in understanding; however, in malice be babes, but **in understanding be mature.*** (1 Corinthians 14:20).

It will take maturity to handle egos, temperaments, emotions, nuances, that are usually expressed in the course of any relationship and work execution.

We learn from Jesus, who is our perfect example, in John 6:70, referring to the disciples, He said; *"Did I not choose you, the twelve, and one of you is a devil?"*

Jesus knew beforehand that Judas was going to betray Him and also that Judas was a thief working against the common wealth and interests of the disciples. Yet, there was no place recorded in the scriptures, where Jesus castigated Judas, put him down or ridiculed him because of his character flaws. He embraced Judas in love just as he embraced the other eleven.

Think about it, if you were privy to an information that your colleague or business partner was going to betray you, you would probably hit the roof, maybe even have a showdown with him.

Jesus understood who Judas was, yet applied God's wisdom, which required maturity in dealing with him. Jesus never discussed Judas with any of the other disciples and did not sack Judas on account of his character. That is maturity, demonstrated by a perfect blend of spirituality (knowing the mind of God on a matter) and wisdom (reasonably adopting the right course of action).

We all know the story of Joseph, how he was sold into slavery by his own brothers. In the course of time, the very same brothers, stood before him, literally at his mercy. He did not pay them back in their own coin but acted in true love. He was spiritual, intelligent, mature, and forgave like a child.

> *But now, do not therefore be grieved or angry with yourselves because you sold me here; for God sent me before you to preserve life (Genesis 45: 5).*

Many times, when God wants to achieve a milestone in your life, He may send you a person or people that would make your current situation extremely uncomfortable and unbearable but will, if handled rightly, enable you birth a certain glory in your life.

He sent Hannah - Peninnah; Joseph - his brothers; David - King Saul. In a lot of instances today, it may even be a spouse. I tell you, it can only end in victory and promotion for you, if you let God's wisdom guide and direct you.

> *And we know that all things work together for good to those who love God, to those who are the called according to His purpose (Romans 8:28)*

Not everyone you live or work with, will like you, speak well of you, work in your best interest or defend you, but it will take your maturity with spirituality, to recognize that God has sent them to you for a purpose, and to work with them, and in spite of them, to achieve God's purpose.

Chapter Eight

Cultivating Your Identity

*Having then gifts differing
according to the grace that is given
to us, let us use them.*
— Romans 12:6

We are familiar with the parable of the talent, wherein three people were given three different amounts of money by their master, before he embarked on a journey (Matthew 25:14-30).

The monies were given with no investment instructions but great expectation of profit.

Whether you have discovered it or not, every person is born with a talent or gift that is expected to be employed to increase the kingdom, and ultimately give glory to God. There are many today who feel they are not good at anything and actually wonder what gifts or talents they may possibly have.

Not everyone will sing like Frank Edwards for example. Not everyone will write like Joyce Meyer. Not everyone will be a charismatic speaker like Barrack Obama. Remember in the parable of the talent, three different people were given three different sums of money. It is God Himself who distributes the talents according to your ability.

Dear child of God, RELAX! The Holy Spirit is an excellent communicator, and can express Himself through any gift or talent, no matter how ordinary or mundane it may appear. He can use your ability to cook, take care of children or even swim, to express Himself.

We are not told if the master in the said parable, spoke to the servants at once or one on one. Maybe the servant who received one talent was aware that his colleagues had received more, and was disgruntled thereby burying his talent.

Never look down on your passion or gifts, no matter how small it may appear relatively. Realize that it is given to you of God and you will give account. The master did not excuse the servant with one talent on the account of the size of the talent. There will always be a time of accountability. If you have not discovered your gift, that thing you are passionate about and enjoy doing, is usually a pointer in the direction of your talent or gift. Look inwards prayerfully and the Holy Spirit will lead you to that gift, which will give you a purpose in life.

Take note, what you receive is not nearly as important as what you do with what you have received. The onus lies on you to discover, nurture, develop and employ your abilities for profit. Everyone is born with a gift, but skill comes from training and development. Your gift/talent is your natural innate ability which is like a diamond in the rough. In its untapped state, it may be unappreciated, though still very valuable. It would have to go through a process to become the valuable gem that is recognized and admired by all.

What are you doing with what you have received? Most times, that natural gift you have will have to go through a process to effectively bless the lives of men. Still on the parable of the talent, the master talked about investing the talent received. Investment, in that context, could also mean application. How are you investing what you have received? If you have a natural flair for cooking, what are you doing to better yourself? Have you invested time in acquiring a wider repertoire of menus, baking, and presentation skills, making cocktails, etc.?

If you recognize God in that gift you have, no matter how insignificant it may appear, the Holy Spirit will work with you and through you, to cultivate that gift and give you a shining identity.

God did not create you to be inactive, so arise dear child of God. Arise from the inactivity. Arise from the depression. Arise from the indecision. Arise from unproductivity.

Isaiah 60:1 urges us to arise and shine. These two instructions will involve identifying your God-given talent, investing it by training, and employing it for profit (the glory of God). When you do this, nations will come to your light and kings to the brightness of your rising (Isaiah 60:3). God Himself will announce you to the world.

Lazy! Wicked! Unprofitable!

The three words are not very complimentary, but they were the master's appraisal of the servant who buried his talent. The action or decision he took to bury the talent did not stem from a lack of knowledge on how to invest the talent but was clearly due to a wrong attitude. Point to note is that the talents were given to these servants in trust, meaning that they would be expected to give account of use. The unproductive servant in response to the master's enquiry, said in verse 24, *"I knew you to be a harsh and hard man, reaping where you did not sow, and gathering where you had not winnowed [the grain]" (AMP)*.

This was the servant's personal opinion of his master. His response suggests that he had certain expectations of his master which were not fulfilled. This gradually led to resentment of the master and a poor attitude towards the master.

Many Christians today, can be likened to the servant who buried his talent. Many have expected God to meet a pressing need in their life, and have developed resentment towards God in words and attitude, and in fact, have "accused" God of being harsh, hard, and demanding.

Example, a couple may have believed God for the fruit of the womb for fifteen years, leading to disappointment, anger and frustration; all of which, in time, may lead to a buildup of resentment towards God. People with these attitude problems "resign" from active state of productivity (bury their talent).

Dear child of God, God is not unrighteous that He will forget and/or overlook your labor of love (Hebrews 6:10). Let your love for the Master keep you aglow with zeal for the work, knowing full well *"that your labor in the Lord is not in vain" (1 Corinthians 15:58 NIV)*, and that you shall prosper in what you do (Psalm 1:3).

Let us look again at the appraisal of the master. It is important to note here, that the servant did not lose that talent. He returned to the master, what was given to him in the same state it was given, hence the master judged him lazy, wicked and unprofitable (worthless).

Living Out God's Purpose and Plan

In verse 30 of that scripture, the unprofitable/worthless servant shared the same consequence of the ungodly.

Another interesting point of note in the theme scripture is fear. In verse 25, the unprofitable servant said, he was afraid, thus he buried the money. A lot of Christians today, are dealing with fear in their lives. Fear of the unknown, fear of how to take the next necessary step, fear of challenges, fear of failure, etc. Fear cripples and can render one lazy, worthless and unproductive. God has instructed over and over again, throughout the bible, "fear not." He gave you the gift or talent because he recognized your capacity/ability. The ability here refers not only to physical ability, but mental, financial and material. Deuteronomy 8:18 says, it is God who gives you the ability to make wealth (profit). Acknowledge always that greater is He that is inside you, than the challenges, recession, inflation, economic downtime and everything else that may try to slow you down or hinder your productivity.

Arise from fear, unearth that talent (if you have buried it already), give yourself to training, be motivated by others who are succeeding in similar endeavors, so that your profiting may be seen by all.

Dear child of God, indeed it is time to arise. Do not ignore or disregard your blessings and gift from God, but invest them wisely and be a blessing.

Good and Faithful

This was yet another appraisal of the master for the other two servants. They were not called good and faithful because of the size of their talents.

1. They recognized that they were entrusted with the talents
2. They invested the talent wisely
3. They saw to it that they made profit

Their ability from the onset, was never in question. However, due to the things they did, they demonstrated responsibility, reliability and a strong sense of accountability. In so doing, they earned an identity and a reputation before the master and the world at large.

Dear child of God, your salvation is not enough. God is looking beyond your salvation to interest/profit (souls). If it were all about your salvation only, God would have no need for you to remain on earth after being born again. You are here for a purpose. Find that purpose and fulfil it.

Benefits of Training

Ignorance is a limitation to productivity. It puts a gap between where you are and where you ought to be.

For optimum productivity, that gap has to be bridged by training.

Why is training so important? Training involves applying yourself through a given process, for a predetermined time period. It requires focus, determination and discipline. Everything in life goes through a period and process of growth and development. God made it so. Training brings about a rich harvest of knowledge, skill and right attitude.

1. **Knowledge**

Albert Einstein said, "Education is not the learning of facts, but the training of the mind to think." Training impacts knowledge. It increases your reasoning ability, mental acumen, and analysis of facts. It helps you think through a problem, challenge the status quo, and bring about necessary solutions in any area of life.

Invest your time wisely: read good books, attend seminars, workshops, conferences, undergo apprenticeship, etc. in your field or areas of interest. It will help increase your mental appreciation of facts, perception and reasoning.

2. **Skill**

Skill is an ability that has been acquired and honed through a period and process of training. It is skill that places a value on your gift and confers an identity on your person. It is the skill that could

Cultivating Your Identity

be referred to as the brightness of your rising as we saw in Isaiah 60:3. The world will come to you, not only because of your gift, but more so, because of your skill. It is the skill that gives the value. Without extensive training, you will never grow to the position of being an effective solution provider.

2 Timothy 3:16-17 (AMP) tells us that amongst other things, that the word of God is given for training in righteousness, so that the man of God may be complete and proficient, well fitted and thoroughly equipped for every good work.

Dear child of God, when you give yourself to training, it makes you complete and proficient, outfitted and thoroughly equipped in any given area.

3. Attitude

Attitude is a complex state involving beliefs, feelings, values and dispositions which makes a person act in certain ways. There are several factors that can affect attitude: background, environment, upbringing, peer group influences and preconceived mindsets. A positive attitude exudes cheerfulness, optimism, joy, hope, etc., while a negative attitude exudes anger, stubbornness, meanness, pride, arrogance, etc.

If you subject yourself to the right training, it will positively impact on your attitude. Remember, we said earlier that training conditions your mind to a renewed way of thinking and reasoning.

Let us take for instance, a medical doctor. The demands of the medical training guarantees value on a human life and will definitely determine the attitude of a medical personnel towards his patients. A bad attitude can completely nullify commendable skill. It is important to note that the right attitude also stems from the value that you yourself have placed on the gift that you have. If you do not recognize the gift as God-given, celebrate and dignify it, whatever skill you may acquire will not be put to much use. There is a saying that it is your attitude (not your skill) that determines your altitude. The right training will definitely bring about an improvement in attitude.

And it is your attitude (not your skill) that births diligence. Diligence observes timelines, exceeds given targets and expectations, and drives excellence in results. Little wonder the bibles says, *"Seest thou a man diligent in his business? he shall stand before kings; he shall not stand before mean men"* (Proverbs 22:29 KJV). Note that this scripture did not say, "Seest thou a man who does business or works" but *"a man diligent in his business or work."* Our Master and our heavenly Boss rewards diligence in our occupations.

Cultivating Your Identity

My wife has over time, been involved in different businesses. At the slightest challenge however, she would abandon the business and look for something "less stressful" to do. When the opportunity came for her to be trained as an entrepreneur, she applied herself, and that training has changed her attitude and results in business.

Your perception by the world and your appraisal by the master will come down to these three important indices:

- Knowledge (what you know)
- Skill (what you can do)
- Attitude (how you do what you do)

When you involve the Holy Spirit in this process, you will definitely make gain/profit in all of your endeavors, and consequently give a commendable state of accounts – *Master, you entrusted me with five talents, see I have gained five talents more.*

Chapter Nine

Exercise Dominion

Then God blessed them, and God said to them, "Be fruitful and multiply; fill the earth and subdue it; have dominion over the fish of the sea, over the birds of the air, and over every living thing that moves on the earth."
— Genesis 1:28

In the theme scripture, we see that God gave man total and absolute dominion – over the fish of the sea, birds of the air and over every living thing that moves on the earth. There was no limit to his jurisdiction. As children of God, we have been raised and made to sit together with Christ, *"far above all principality and power and might and dominion, and every name that is named"* (Ephesians 1:21). This scripture tells us that we are seated in the place of dominion and absolute authority. Therefore, we should never be victims of circumstances, but rather rule over circumstances. Our circumstances should never define who we are. This can only happen when we exercise our authority.

Take Nigeria for instance, although extremely blessed, she is regarded by the world as backward, undeveloped, corrupt and poverty stricken. As a result, generally, the first thing an outsider will see of a Nigerian, is not a man with great potential, who has the capacity of turning the world around, but a man held down by the negativity of his environment. This explains the large exodus of Nigerians from the country, in an attempt to seek a better environment for their "success." The question is really not how to migrate from their environment to become successful in life, but how you and I will take charge and change our environment. The very first step should not be about getting a conducive environment to develop yourself and succeed, but rather, first develop yourself, harness your strengths and potentials, then change your environment.

> *For behold, darkness shall cover the earth,*
> *and dense darkness [all] peoples, but the*
> *Lord shall arise upon you [O Jerusalem],*

and His glory shall be seen on you (Isaiah 60:2 AMP).

The scripture above tells us that darkness covers the earth, and deep darkness covers the people. The darkness of corruption, poverty, recession, hardship, inflation, injustice and cruelty covers the government, institutions, organizations, families, politics, and different sectors of the economy. This is a wake-up call. Things will not get better for you, so do not wait for the environment, policies or the economy to improve to support your dreams and aspirations.

Still in that scripture, we understand that the Lord will rise upon you, not upon the government, not upon the private sector but on you, and His glory and brilliance will be seen on you. The question is, will you let Him rise upon you? The Lord will only rise when you arise.

Defy the Environment

The very popular Bill Gates, is a billionaire today, not because he had the privilege of a conducive environment to launch his business. He must have faced challenges in creating Microsoft – the computer programming software as we know it today. He forged ahead in spite of challenges faced, and today the world in general is a better place because he refused to take no for an answer.

Another example is the very beautiful Queen Esther. During the reign of her husband King Ahasuerus (Xerxes), there was a law that every man or woman who came to the king without being summoned would be put to death. Now there was a matter of great urgency for which the queen needed to seek audience with her husband. The law did not exempt her as queen, she needed to be summoned just as any other citizen. Note her response to Mordecai, her uncle, in Esther 4:11b, *"And as for me I have not been summoned to come to the king for these last thirty days."* However, she recognized that she served the living God who is sovereign in the affairs of men. She made up her mind to take that step of faith – then I will go in to see the king (without being summoned), which is against the law; and if I perish, I perish (Esther 4:16).

Dear child of God, have confidence in God and who you are in Christ. Even if the government policies, environmental factors and circumstances, work to stop you, refuse to be stopped. Refuse to be defined by your environment and circumstances. Take charge and develop your God-given potentials and talents.

Stay Above

An American president, John F. Kennedy, in his inaugural address, spoke his famous words, "Ask not what your country can do for you, ask what you can do for your country." In others words, do not let the government of your country limit your potential.

When you have a renewed mindset, you are confident that you can never be limited or defined by your country. With diligence and consistency, you would end up being in position, not only to be a blessing to your country but others as well.

> *However, there should not be any poor among you, for the LORD will surely bless you in the land that he is giving you as an inheritance, if you carefully obey him by keeping all these commandments that I am giving you today. For the LORD your God will bless you just as he has promised; you will lend to many nations but will not borrow from any, and you will rule over many nations but they will not rule over you (Deuteronomy 15:4-6 NET).*

As a child of God, you are blessed to be a blessing. You have no business struggling. There are principles in the bible for prosperity and productivity.

Though Jesus said to His disciples, *"You have the poor with you always"* (Matt 26:11), He was referring to those Christians who would likely shun or refuse instructions (for their prosperity).

Your prosperity and productivity are tied to your walking in the God-given principles for prosperity. That is your guarantee for exercising dominion over struggle, poverty and hardship. Like Noah's ark, life's challenges will not sink or overwhelm you, but rather provide opportunities for your lifting and promotion. Note, as the ark was built to the Lord's specification, likewise our lives, families and business endeavors, should be established according to God's specification in order to remain above only.

Build That Ark

In Genesis chapter 6, to preserve the life of Noah and his family, God instructed Noah to build an ark that will save him from the flood. Noah obeyed God's instruction to the letter. The heavy rains and flood destroyed all life in existence, but bore Noah's ark up.

What has God instructed you to build? For Noah, it was an ark. For you, it may be building your spirit, your character, your gifts and potentials. The very thing God has asked you to build, improve on, maximize through training and discipline, could very well be the thing that will keep you afloat, when the floods of life come. In Noah's time, no mountain or tall building, was safe from the flood. All the tree tops were covered by the flood.

Today, we hear of some of the Fortune 500 companies that have sunk due to recession, economic downtime, etc. If such economic giants can fail, it is very clear then, that your success and prosperity can only be in Christ, and in "building the ark" that He has instructed you to build. One man's ark differs from the other.

Your ark could be something as basic as building your family, or something enterprising as establishing business partnerships, getting franchise, or something educational as getting a new degree or certification, or relating to investments like buying land, starting a savings, etc. It could even be as fundamental as paying attention to your health and wellbeing: changing your diet, exercising to remain healthy and fit, etc.

Every man is expected by God to build. Discover yours and start building right away.

Reign with Words

Where the word of a king is, there is power (Ecclesiastes 8:4a).

The bible refers to Christians, as kings and priests unto God (Revelation 5:10).

From the above scripture, we see that kings reign by their words. As children of God, we also reign in life by our words, not by our natural birth and pedigree, education or by our salaries or income.

The fact that you are born again does not translate to instant success. You need to be able to dominate your world by your tongue and through your words.

> *Death and life are in the power of the tongue, and those who love it and indulge it will eat its fruit and bear the consequences of their words (Proverbs 18:21 AMP).*

No matter what you may face in life, be very careful what you say. You can build your life up or tear it down by the words you speak. Never talk poverty, defeat, sickness or death, for life is spiritual. Always speak what God has said concerning you and your situation. Never say "I cannot do it", "I am not qualified", "life is hard", "this country is bad", etc. The bible says you will have whatever you say (Mark 11:23).

As you make declarations of faith daily, the Lord will lead you to take the right steps in maximizing your potentials – trainings, skill acquisitions, apprenticeship, collaboration, etc. for faith without works is dead.

Are You Known?

For those of you who have commenced work, effectively using your gift and talents to bless lives, the question is, are you known for what you do?

Let us take a look at the young boy David. He was sent by his father to deliver food to his brothers who were soldiers in Israel and at the time fighting the Philistines. As he was talking to his brothers, Goliath came out to threaten the army of Israel. David did not keep silent, he was busy making enquiries from the soldiers about the situation, as well as making faith-filled declarations. He said, for who is this uncircumcised Philistine that has taunted and defiled the armies of the living God (1 Samuel 17:26b). When the words that David spoke were heard, the men reported the words to Saul the king, and David was thereby summoned by the king.

Please note, that it was the confident boast of David that brought him before the king. If he had said nothing, he would never have been known.

This is where the power of advertisement comes in; the power of media. Thank God for social platforms like WhatsApp, Instagram, Facebook, Twitter, blog, etc. From wherever you are, you can sell yourself to the world. It does not matter what you do. Even if you sell a commodity like "garri" (processed cassava), you can lift this trade several notches higher by selling value. You can bag the garri, brand it and advertise on social media with added services of home delivery at a premium.

Refuse to be small. Work on yourself and your brand. Ensure that you attain a standard and quality, such as you can export beyond your immediate environment. Celebrate your brand, create awareness, constantly research to see what others offering the same services are doing, and do better.

The quality of your product or service is not sufficient in itself to give you widespread awareness and recognition. Make use of your immediate sphere of contacts (direct marketing, advertising on social platforms, using physical media of advertisements through fliers, and the media when necessary) to be seen and heard.

The Land Flowing with Milk and Honey

> *So I have come down to deliver them out of the hand of the Egyptians, and to bring them up from that land to **a good and large land**, to **a land flowing with milk***

and honey, *to the place of the Canaanites and the Hittites and the Amorites and the Perizzites and the Hivites and the Jebusites (Exodus 3:8-9).*

This was the land promised to the children of Israel. It was a good and large land. From the above scripture, we see that it was not just another type of Eden, prepared and kept to be inhabited by Israelites alone. The bible tells us that it was a land already occupied by other nations. In other words, it was a land of opportunity, yet associated with risks.

To occupy and enjoy this land, the Israelites needed to first, physically engage the occupants and drive them out. Second, upon securing the land for themselves, they needed to cultivate the land to yield fruits.

It is important to pause here for a moment and ponder. The description *"flowing with milk and honey"* was given before the Israelite occupied that land. The land was flowing with milk and honey and enjoyed by a people who did not know God.

For the Israelites to enjoy the good of the land, they had to work the land like the occupants before them, to enjoy its productivity. The land would not produce or yield for them, simply because God was with them. They had to apply their acquired skills as farmers to enjoy the same benefits.

Having God with them, and for them, was an added advantage for their productivity and security in that land.

The term, *"flowing with milk and honey"*, did not suggest a life of idleness and a false sense of entitlement. It meant that the land was fruitful and when cultivated would yield abundantly.

Maybe God has pointed out your own land flowing with milk and honey. For me it is writing. For you, it could be nursing, teaching or singing. And the fact that God is in it, does not mean it will not have challenges.

Writing for me, is a *"land flowing with milk and honey"*. In the world of writing already, there are numerous gifted and successful writers, who are enjoying outstanding recognition and success as writers.

A lot of these successful writers are not Christians writing faith inspired books, but are succeeding all the same with a large base of readers worldwide. I cannot dominate in this world, solely on the basis of being a Christian. To be able to favorably compete, and be relevant in this world, I need to acquire relevant skills and proficiencies, which will come through training, mentorship, collaboration and reading vast.

My being a Christian whose work is inspired by the Holy Ghost Himself, will definitely give me the required advantage of staying on top and ahead when I have done all I am required to do.

The Door of Opportunity

The Israelites were farmers in Egypt, who never had the need for the art and skills of war in Egypt. Can you imagine what would have happened to them if they had not acquired the skill by training themselves to fight? They would have been overpowered and overwhelmed by the enemy.

There will always be related skills or strategies to employ in the course of doing your work. Example, advertising in the place of business is one of the needed strategies, collaboration is another (the soldiers of Israel did not fight alone in possessing the land; they fought together).

You will realize, that as you pursue that God given talent, several more avenues for self-development and capacity building will arise, to make you a consummate individual and brand.

> *For a wide door of opportunity for effectual [service] has opened to me [there, a great and promising one], and [there are] many adversaries (1 Corinthians 16:9 AMP)*

The Lord opened a wide door (a very promising opportunity for Paul) and yet there were many adversaries for him to overcome. So, the fact that God is in it does not mean it will be easy. These adversaries (challenges, oppositions) are basically opportunities for your growth and development as a person and brand.

Stay focused. Stay on course. The problems or challenges we face in the course of the work, serve to bring out the best of us for greater productivity.

Observing Right Practices

Not only did the Israelites have to rely on farming and fighting skills, there were other factors that came to play in settling successfully in the land of Canaan. Security systems, health practices, right diet, keeping the sabbath, etc. were things that had to come into play in the normal course of living.

God made rest mandatory for the Israelites. In fact, keeping the seventh day was a law. The Lord Himself gave us a perfect example. In the course of creation, He rested on the seventh day. He didn't rest because He was tired or worn out by creation. NO! He has given us an example to live by.

Don't jettison rest because you need to meet a deadline, or because you feel the body can be pushed further. Take out time daily to rest and refresh yourself. Don't skip meals.

There was also time to give the land some rest from cultivation. Plan a vacation with your family yearly. It will help in bonding with your spouse and children. It also rejuvenates you, physically, mentally and emotionally.

Dear child of God, in the bid to make a living, DO NOT FORGET TO LIVE.

What Is in Your Hand?

We should never rule out the place of miracles in our lives, families, business, endeavors, etc. However, that does not mean that you do nothing and wait for God to do everything for you. Acquire the basics – knowledge, training, skills in building your God-given potentials, and God will bless it supernaturally. God does not bless emptiness. He will always require something from you that He can bless.

We all know the miracle of the feeding of the five thousand (Matthew 14:13-21). Jesus did not create those loaves of bread and fish. The five loaves and two fish as we know, were a little boy's lunch. The disciples brought the very meager meal to Jesus, to feed five thousand men, besides women and children. Compared to the very many mouths to feed, this lunch was grossly inadequate. From the story, we establish that Jesus blessed it and invoked into it the power to multiply supernaturally. Consequently, it was more than enough to satisfy the thousands of people present.

Always have something in your hand that God can increase supernaturally. Basic mathematics tells us that any number multiplied by zero is zero. God will involve you to do great things with you, through you and for you. You are the miracle that the world is waiting for today. The bible says that all *"creation waits for the manifestation of the sons of God"* (Romans 8:19).

Dear child of God, come out of obscurity. Manifest yourself. Be a blessing. Be a miracle. It starts with you.

Keep It Real

We all hear testimonies of how people receive sudden promotion in life. A position they did not plan or work for. We call them miracles and I am a strong believer in miracles.

A lot of times, the miracles are really opportunities given by God to grow, develop, and make impact in your world. I am certain you have heard of people who were going through a lot of challenges in life. Suddenly, out of the blues, they were given a political appointment, or awarded a contract that took them out of the poverty bracket.

Sadly, however a lot of people have turned these promotions to be all about themselves. They become self-centred, rude, pompous and arrogant.

A young maiden in bible times, experienced a similar and sudden promotion that changed her life forever. We all know the story of Esther, a beautiful slave girl. She probably had no aspirations for greatness, but due to a very high-powered divine manoeuvre, she found herself to be the king's delight and bride.

The new Queen Esther certainly enjoyed the privileges of royalty. Little did she know that the promotion and privilege were not about her but for the deliverance of an entire nation. Mordecai, her uncle, reminded her of this when he said in Esther 4:14b, *"And who knows but that you have come to the kingdom for such a time as this and for this very occasion?" (AMP).*

With this wakeup call, Esther immediately refocused and realigned herself to God's purpose for her in that exalted position.

Dear child of God, your experience may not be on the same scale with Esther, but if you have received any promotion, especially one you were not prepared for or worked for, do not be overwhelmed by the perks of the position. Realize very quickly, that God has a reason for it. God is not a waster of opportunities or resources. Make good use of that opportunity/promotion. Build on it, improve yourself to ensure lasting success and greater impact.

When that season (appointment or office or job) ends, have you been able to put structures on ground (intellectual structures, financial structures, physical structures, academic structures) to ensure continuous productivity?

Dear child of God, be wise. Make maximum use of your time, opportunities and promotions.

Do not live for yourself. Be a blessing to your family and members of the household of faith (Galatians 6:10).

Certainly, you will give account of every promotion and opportunity God brings your way.

Chapter Ten

Stay Focused

Do you not know that those who run in a race all run, but one receives the prize? Run in such a way that you may obtain it.
—1 Corinthians 9:24

Nowadays, life seems to be on the fast lane, with men having little to zero tolerance for waiting or pausing. Everything seems to be on the go. We have fast-food options, drive through cafés, internet-based banking transactions, fast mail delivery, online shopping, etc. It is lovely to have everything that you desire at the snap of your fingers, but in life, there is a time, season and process for everything.

A woman having waited fifteen years in her marital home to have a child, will not just conceive and deliver in thirty days, she will have to go through the full process of time expected for child birth.

As Christians, we are entitled to the birthright of prosperity and success, but we are responsible to make it happen.

Everything you require to succeed is inside of you. *"His divine power has given to us all things that pertain to life and godliness"* (2 Peter 1:3).

Through focus, discipline and diligence you are expected to harness all of your strengths and competences to make good success in life.

Proverbs 13:11 says, *"Wealth [not earned but] won in haste will dwindle away, but he who gathers little by little will increase [his riches]"* (AMP) (paraphrased).

If you are a tailor for instance, do not expect that in six months to one year you would have grown so big, gained a lot of patronage, and probably employed more staff due to demand. If you refuse to be discouraged, and stay true to the task, you will indeed grow steadily and be very successful.

Peter experienced a bout of uncertainty, fear, frustration and discouragement, when Jesus was taken away from them, arrested and crucified. Jesus represented to Peter and the other disciples, security, certainty, safety, provision, and protection. Jesus was the reason the disciples stayed together in this "new occupation of fishers of men."

Understandably, with their mentor, support system, teacher, and guide gone, Peter may have felt unanchored and vulnerable, so decided to go back to his comfort zone. A life and occupation that he understood completely, and was well prepared for.

Dear child of God, refuse to be overwhelmed by the challenges and pressures of life. Refuse to be pushed to the point where you opt to do that which God has not instructed you to do, merely because you feel it is a safer option with a surer promise of profit.

> *Seest thou a man diligent in his business? he shall stand before kings; he shall not stand before mean men (Proverbs 22:29 KJV).*

From the above scripture, we can see that it is not the nature of your job that guarantees success. So, it does not matter if you are a doctor, singer, painter or bricklayer. It is the quality of your attitude, your commitment, your tenacity and doggedness towards the work you do that matters.

Dear child of God, in that business you do, are you diligent? The word diligent means to be attentive, meticulous, persevering, tireless and hardworking. If your attitude is right towards the work you do, it will only be a matter of time before you are well known, successful and indispensable because of the product or service you offer.

Your greatest competition should not be your friend or neighbor, but rather, your past achievements. It is very wrong to compare yourself with others. You are on a very different path in life, stay on your course and be focused.

If you do not tire or give up, you will indeed stand before kings – be in high demand, well known, successful, respected and famous.

There are notable men in ministry and secular work, who through patience, perseverance, and hard work have become outstanding successes and examples for us to follow.

Today, we hear of Bill Gates, Aliko Dangote and some of our great men in the faith; Pastor Sam Adeyemi, T D Jakes, Kenneth Hagin. The list is endless.

These men have grown steadily, through decades of hard work, perseverance and diligence to become the icons we know today.

Let us look at a man I admire a lot, Joseph. He was appointed Prime Minister in Egypt. We know from the scriptures, that under his tenure as prime minister, Egypt grew stronger economically. They had more than enough grain that the whole world depended on Egypt for their supply. In today's economic parlance, we can say that Egypt was strong in foreign exchange.

Their colossal economic status was not attained in the first or second year of Joseph's appointment. We understand that the first seven years of his appointment, were years of plenty, which he converted to years of investments and savings.

After seven years, he took advantage of the global economic downturn, and sold the grains he had taken seven years to gather. Apart from the Egyptians, no one had probably ever heard of Joseph during the seven years of abundance. However, he became relevant and indispensable in the course of time, because he gave attention to the business at hand, for seven full years.

Dear child of God, make sure that through your strengths and your gifts, you are meeting a need in life. Develop yourself and be the best at what you are.

Be diligent and focused, and you too will become indispensable.

Recognize Opportunity

Someone reading this book may probably be wondering, does not all this teaching kick out the essence of multiple streams of income, the need to be multidimensional? Does it not limit lateral self-development? It is commonly said today that to be successful, you need to have multiple streams of revenue. I agree totally, and this was discussed in the third chapter.

The Holy Spirit is dynamic. In the course of your work, He may bring to you opportunities, business ideas, business contacts/alliances. You need to follow the leading of the Holy Spirit, and prayerfully explore opportunities that come your way. This however does not mean that you will be distracted from your core occupation. God may just be bringing your way other avenues to make deeper impact. Do not be stereotyped in life. It stifles growth and creativity.

I recognize that I now have an occupation of writing, but that does not mean God will not open up other opportunities for me to be blessed and be a blessing.

When God instructed Philip to meet with the Ethiopian eunuch, there was no verbal instruction to have the eunuch baptized. However, Philip and the eunuch saw and recognized an opportunity to have the eunuch baptized, and seized it.

The point here is to put all opportunities within context, with the sole aim and purpose to bring God glory, as well as better the lives of people in your world.

Note that if you develop an interest that takes your attention away from God, and your divine purpose or mission on earth, you will not stand the test of time. The people who built the tower of babel had a wrong motive. They enjoyed relative success for a time, as the building rose from the foundation level to become almost an edifice. Since it did not work for the glory of

God, it was never completed. God was not against the process or occupation of building, but the building was not centered on Him. Consequently, God did not take away their potentials and skills as builders, but rather the enabling environment (common language), for a successful completion of the project.

Any preoccupation, interest, job, project, career, relationship, partnership that is not centered on God, can be likened to building a tower of babel. Ensure that you are not involved in building your own tower of babel. Set your mind on kingdom matters.

Wait for the Instruction

People get frustrated when, out of impatience (feeling that they are ready and fully equipped to meet a need), they step out of the place of training and perseverance. It is like offering half baked bread to the public. They may come for it the first time but will definitely not give you repeat business.

We are very familiar with the story of Peter's first encounter with Jesus in Luke 5:1-4. Jesus had asked Peter to push his boat away from the land, so that He (Jesus), could speak to the multitude. Peter obeyed.

Interestingly, Peter not only obeyed, but sat in the boat with Jesus, for the entire duration of His ministration. The bible records that when Jesus had stopped speaking, He instructed Peter to let down his net for a harvest.

Let us analyze this together. We understand from the scripture, that Peter had labored from sun down to sun up and caught nothing. Understandably, he was tired, hungry, disappointed and cranky. He could have pushed the boat into the water and gone back to continue washing his nets, or better still, find something to eat. He did no such thing, but patiently sat with Jesus in the boat.

Jesus did not give him the instruction to let down the net at the onset or during the course of His preaching, but when He had stopped speaking, He told Peter to launch out.

Has the Holy Spirit certified that you have garnered the requisite trainings and skills for you to launch out? Has He Himself given you the instruction to launch out or are you doing it on your own? The bible says, *"Not by might nor by power, but by My Spirit, says the Lord of hosts"* (Zechariah 4:6).

Dear child of God, the Word of God and the Holy Spirit are your guaranteed advantage in business. This is what will sustain you in your business and keep you ahead of competition. It was the relationship Daniel and his friends had with God, that made them ten times better than their peers.

> *And in all matters of wisdom and understanding about which the king examined them, he found them **ten times***

> ***better*** *than all the magicians and astrologers who were in all his realm (Daniel 1:20).*

It is also important to note, that Daniel and his friends had submitted themselves to a three-year intensive training, before serving the king as advisers (Daniel 1:5). They went through this training together with several other recruits but they stood out because of their added advantage – God.

Let God into every step of your plans and learn to listen for His voice. If you launch out at the right time, you will find a world ready and willing for your products, services and message.

What Are Your Add-Ons?

> *But also for this very reason, giving all diligence, add to your faith virtue, to virtue knowledge, to knowledge self-control, to self-control perseverance, to perseverance godliness, to godliness brotherly kindness, and to brotherly kindness love. For if these things are yours and abound, you will be*

> *neither barren nor unfruitful in the knowledge of our Lord Jesus Christ (2 Peter 1:5-8).*

So, you know how to cook, write, or sew, praise God!

These gifts or potentials in themselves, are not enough to guarantee outstanding success. The theme scripture says add to your faith virtue, and then mentioned a range of add-ons which will guarantee that you will neither be barren nor unfruitful in the knowledge of our Lord Jesus Christ.

Simply put, faith is not enough! What are you adding to your gift or potential to ensure that you are neither barren nor unfruitful in your business? Have you added training, research, mentorship, apprenticeship, collaboration? Are you still dreaming of hitting the jackpot with just raw potential?

The world is becoming intensely competitive. Staying relevant will require a life of continuous discipline and self-improvement.

Joseph's gift got him before the king, but that gift alone did not earn him the position of Prime Minister. It was the wisdom of his "sound economic policies" that secured him the second highest position in Egypt (Genesis 4:25-41).

So, where did Joseph learn this remarkable business intelligence and acumen? In Potiphar's house and in prison, he was made the overseer of all the affairs (Gen 39:6,23). There he learned relationship skills, management of human, physical and financial resources, as well as negotiating and investment skills. All of these add-ons made Joseph a consummate business and economic veteran.

If you know how to cook for instance, know that this in itself, cannot run and sustain a viable restaurant business. Apart from training, which is fundamental, you need to understand food as a business: risks and mitigations, book keeping, customer care, vendor management, food preservation, payment systems, public relations, etc.

You must constantly stay one step ahead of competition by rendering incomparable service delivery. As you can see, you will require a lot of add-ons to your talent of cooking.

It is not only the quality of food that will ensure repeat business for you. The location, ambience, service, attitude of staff, etc. will ensure that your business and your brand grow steadily over time.

Stay Updated

Let us take a look again, at the great man Joseph. The Egyptians, during the seven years of famine, also used their lands to barter for the grains Joseph sold. At a point, Joseph had bought up all the land in Egypt.

After the seven years of famine, he identified another business opportunity. He leased the said lands back to the Egyptians at a lease rental agreement of a portion of whatever the land produced.

Consequently, Pharaoh's treasury grew steadily from the lease rentals and the grains (Genesis 47:13-26). Joseph's business acumen enabled him to identify an emerging business opportunity and harness it. This could not have come about by the ability to dream and interpret dreams alone.

Dear child of God, needs evolve over time. A business runs the risk of being outdated, irrelevant or obsolete. If you do not stay abreast of trends, changes and seasons, and tailor your services to stay relevant, the business may become extinct. There was a time when one depended on professional photographers to take good pictures. Today, phones have been upgraded to have high definition cameras and autofocus thus reducing the dependency on photographers.

For photography studios to stay relevant in business, they have to outsmart and outdo what the phone cameras can do – providing various options of background, props, lighting etc. Now the studios can produce photobooks which are better and more durable than albums that were available previously.

Importance of Certification

In any field or scope of work, while it is important to be self-aware and self-confident – believing in the quality of your brand, it is also equally very important, to be endorsed authoritatively as having met certain professional or work requirements/standards. This however does not mean leaning on the opinion of others concerning your work, but it brings fulfillment to you as a professional, that you are qualified to compete with the very best in the field.

The world is becoming increasingly discriminative, with zero tolerance for mediocrity. People would rather pay that extra premium for assured quality and competence. It is therefore very important to ambitiously acquire the relevant trainings and certifications in your field of work. This will shore up the confidence level of prospective patrons because it will be officially on record that you are certified to perform a specified function, or practice a particular skill.

In Daniel 1:20, we remember that Daniel and his friends were **examined** by the king (who represented the highest authority in endorsement of skill). By comparative analysis, they were found to be ten times better than their peers. This was not Daniel's self-assessment but an external assessment, which enabled him clinch a more reputable position of standing before the king and serving him personally.

There are opportunities that may never come to you until you put yourself through specific training to obtain specific qualifications in your field of work. So, raise your sight. Continuously seek to do better than your past, and nothing can stop you.

Coaching

Dear child of God, ability can either be enhanced or dissipated by company. Who you are talking or listening to is very important. It will determine how far you will go in any area of your life. Samson's great ability and ministry was brought to a premature and very sad end, because he got entangled with the wrong company.

This takes me to a field of sports celebrated world wide – football. To a very large extent, the team's performance is a reflection of the quality of coaching received. Let us take a very well celebrated coach: Zinedine Zidane. He has been voted the world's best coach. The Real Madrid's outstanding performances (three back to back UEFA championships) were a direct reflection of this man's coaching abilities and prowess.

The importance of coaching cannot be overemphasized. If you do not have a coach (mentor) currently, you need to prayerfully be guided to getting one.

So, what is coaching? It is all about unlocking potential, maximizing performance and helping the coachee by direct participation, involvement and dynamic interaction. All of these will in turn have a direct and positive impact on your work, performance or results.

Let us take an example of someone from the bible, who benefited immensely from the presence of a "coach" in her life. The book of Ruth tells us the story of a young widow, Ruth the Moabitess. It is on record, that the young lady followed her mother-in-law, Naomi, to a land, people, culture and customs that were alien to her. We understand from the scriptures that once they arrived Bethlehem, Naomi took Ruth under her wings. She gave Ruth series of advice and counsel through her dynamic interaction and involvement with Ruth. This led Ruth to be chosen by Boaz, a God-fearing and very eligible bachelor in his time. Our Lord Jesus Christ was a descendant of this very blessed union. If Ruth did not have a coach or mentor in Naomi, she may never have featured in the genealogy of our Lord Jesus Christ.

Dear child of God, take this very delicate matter to the Lord in prayer. He will guide you into having that specific person that will work with you in building and enhancing your abilities.

Have a Succession Plan

Having been mentored, coached or raised and experienced outstanding success in your chosen field, what are your plans for continuity? You cannot be said to have succeeded in life, without having raised, mentored or coached a successor.

If you are not replicating your success in the life of another, then all of your years of achievements, accomplishments and success have indeed come to naught.

Today we see business empires, families, and even ministries crumble, because there was no one entrusted to take that project to the next and higher level. God is interested in a succession plan. That is why he instructed us to go into the world and make disciples of the nations.

When God informed David that he would not build the temple, can you imagine what would have happened if Solomon was not groomed in place? It is important to understand that Solomon was not the only son. In fact, he was not the first son, the heir to the throne. However, he was the son that had been mentored by his father, David.

> *My son, hear the instruction of your father,*
> *and do not forsake the law of your mother;*
> *For they will be a graceful ornament on*

> *your head, and chains about your neck (Proverb 1:8-9).*

> *Only may the Lord give you wisdom and understanding, and give you charge concerning Israel, that you may keep the law of the Lord your God. Then you will prosper, if you take care to fulfill the statutes and judgments with which the Lord charged Moses concerning Israel. Be strong and of good courage; do not fear nor be dismayed (1 Chronicles 22:12-13).*

Solomon had earned the reputation of a successor before God, that is why God could entrust him with the very important task/commission of building the temple. In addition, David proactively made provision of gold, silver, bronze, iron, timber, and stone for Solomon to use when the time came (1 Chronicles 22:14). He trusted that Solomon would judiciously use these resources and not put them to waste. Why? He had been mentored and coached by David.

When God gives you a responsibility or task, be so good at it, that you can invest your wealth of knowledge and experience in a succession plan. This will guarantee that your work and results will still be speaking and making impacts in the lives of generations of men, long after you are gone.

Be Wary of Dream Killers

When God gives you a vision or dream, first own it and internalize it. The fact that it is God-given does not mean that everyone will believe in it or support you. Sometimes, the very people you expect to excitedly back you up, and encourage you in your God-given dreams are the very ones who will not only adopt a position of indifference, but will actively oppose you and openly fight you. At such times, it is how much confidence you have in God's grace and ability, to fulfil His dream and purpose in your life, that will actually determine if it succeeds or fails. Very well-known bible figures come to mind - David and Joseph.

David, who was the youngest son of his father was sent by his father, to deliver some provisions to the first three sons who had enlisted in King Saul's army. When he arrived, he heard Goliath challenge the army of Israel, and right away began to make enquiries in his quest to destroy Goliath. In 1 Samuel 17:28, we see that his older brother, Eliab, openly lost his temper and attacked David. He ignored his older brother, refused to be intimidated or shut down, and went ahead to destroy Goliath and gained victory for Israel.

God gave Joseph a dream of leadership, which he shared with his parents and brothers. He was scorned and ridiculed by the very people that he had hoped would encourage and support him.

As you can see, dear child of God, if you are experiencing any confrontation concerning God's purpose in your life, you are not alone. It hurts even more when the very ones closest to you are working against you. Oh yes! It may even be your spouse, your pastor, leader or boss, but *set your face as a flint* and refuse to be moved.

Pay no heed to the voices of anger, false accusation, ridicule, mockery or scorn. Forge ahead. Do not flag in zeal. Let the zeal of the work consume you. Be fervent in spirit, serving the Lord. Sooner or later, those who laughed at you or resisted you, will join you in serving the Lord, if you do not lose heart.

Chapter Eleven

Phases of Execution

> *For which of you, intending to build a tower, does not sit down first and count the cost, whether he has enough to finish it — lest, after he has laid the foundation, and is not able to finish, all who see it begin to mock him, saying, 'This man began to build and was not able to finish.'*
> *— Luke 14:28-30*

From the above scripture, we quickly see that it is a stigma, a thing of ridicule, to start a good thing and not have the ability, competence or resources to finish it. There is a cost to every endeavor, work or project in life.

When we hear the word "cost", what immediately comes to mind is a financial implication. Very true. However, over and beyond financial cost, which is very important in starting any project, there are several other costs to be applied – intellectual cost, competence/skill cost, time cost, human resources cost, etc.

Dear child of God, as you go ahead with that task or endeavor, ensure that you have calculated every cost implication. The bible says that, *"The end of a thing is better than its beginning"* (Ecclesiastes 7:8).

Our heavenly Father is a finisher. Hebrews 12:2 describes Him as, *"The author and finisher (perfection) of our faith" (paraphrased).* Consequently, it behooves us, as children of God, to imitate God as finishers, for **it is the finished product that brings glory to the master**.

I had said earlier, in previous chapters, that there is time and process in every sphere of work. Let us learn from the Master Himself. Everything about creation was strategic and in phases. God Himself went through different phases in creation, starting from the brooding phase.

Brooding Phase

> *The earth was without form and an empty waste, and darkness was upon the face of the very great deep. The **Spirit of God was** moving (hovering, **brooding**) over the face of the waters (Genesis 1:2 AMP).*

What does it mean to brood? – meditate, dwell on, mutter. The bible describes a bleak situation in Genesis 1:2 – chaos, darkness and emptiness. Interestingly, in the midst of the chaos, the Spirit of God was present.

The fact that the task is assigned to you by God, does not mean there will not be challenges. If you intend to start a project, or seek to solve an identified problem, approach it the same way our Father did, meditatively.

In this phase, you are getting to know all the short-term and long-term goals and requirements for your business or project. You may also get to note the challenges you will face in embarking on the project, then take this up in prayer.

Even if you may have the capital available, do not jump in to start. This is the time to search the scriptures, or meditate on those specific things that God has spoken concerning the project or your dream.

I encourage you to spend time praying, and seeking the face of God concerning the dream or project you want to embark on. Call that project by name, get to understand all the requirements for the project, meditate on the word and allow God throw more light on the project.

This is not the time to speak out concerning your project. You are still in the brooding stage or phase. As you meditate, the Lord will give you ideas, will bring creative thoughts to you, give you a mental picture or strategies on how to begin. Note them or write them down.

Let us look at the account of the woman with the flow of blood:

> *And suddenly, a woman who had a flow of blood for twelve years came from behind and touched the hem of His garment. For **she said to herself**, "If only I may touch His garment, I shall be made well"* (Matthew 9:20-21)

The woman needed healing. She had spent all her savings on doctors, but there was no cure. She knew Christ as healer and decided to embark on a journey of faith. Before she took the first step literally, she brooded. She said to herself, *"If only I may touch His garment, I shall be made well."* That touch ended up drawing out healing power from Jesus that got her healed instantly. Notice that this healing started by brooding which shored up her faith in Jesus. Before she took that first step, she was convinced that she would have a testimony.

Faith comes by hearing, and hearing by the word of God (Romans 10:17). In her brooding, the woman received a strategy on how to obtain her healing.

> *Call to Me, and I will answer you, and show you great and mighty things, which you do not know. (Jeremiah 33:3)*

Similarly, in the midst of the problems, challenges and chaos, the Spirit of God is present. As you pray and meditate, He will give you outstanding ideas on how to get the problems solved. These ideas are not ordinary ideas but inspired by the Holy Ghost for your success. No matter how large or how numerous the problems are, you are assured of victory.

At this stage, God gives you a note of victory through specific words. Once you receive this note of victory in your spirit, then the time has come to speak.

Speaking Phase

In this phase of execution, you are making declarations concerning every aspect of your business or project. Declarations of victory, provision, favor, supernatural help, productivity and profitability.

This speaking stage will be sustained throughout the life of your business, because we understand that life is spiritual, and the power of life and death lies in the tongue (Proverbs 18:21).

In this phase, begin to put things in place. Make the necessary contacts, enquiries, applications where necessary. Have your plan and ensure that it is aligned with God's specific idea or vision given to you.

> *Then the Lord answered me and said: "Write the vision and make it plain on tablets, that he may run who reads it"* (Habakkuk 2:2).

I love the phrase in the scripture above that says *"that he may run who reads it."* This is very instructive. It instructs that we should make the vision actionable, in such a way that when you read it, it gives you a sense of purpose and direction, prompting and propelling you to take necessary and decisive steps towards actualization.

An effective plan should have;

- the goal or task
- timeline for completion
- the responsible party where necessary
- and status updates

You cannot go to a bank or a financial institution, for instance, to ask for a loan without a business plan. You will never be taken seriously.

At this point, you are working out your faith. No matter how you have meditated and prayed, all of that becomes void if you do not match them to the right steps and planning. And God is interested in your plans, so that he can be involved in it.

> *A man's heart plans his way, but the Lord directs his steps (Proverbs 16:9).*

In addition to the short-term plans or goals that will take your business or project from the point of startup to the next level, you must also have, midterm and long-term plans or goals. This does not apply in business only, but also in your personal life and even marriage.

Some extremists may counter this, on the strength of argument in the scripture of James 4:14, *"Whereas you do not know what will happen tomorrow. For what is your life? It is even a vapor that appears for a little time and then vanishes away."*

So, if we are not sure of tomorrow, one may ask, why do we need to plan our lives, business, and families five, ten years from today? Even God Himself is a long-term planner.

When God addressed Jeremiah, He told him that before Jeremiah was formed in the womb, He (God) had plans for Jeremiah (Jeremiah 1:5).

There are several other scriptures that show us that God endorses plans and deliberateness of actions.

God gave Joshua a plan and strategy to take over Jericho as seen in Joshua chapter 6.

When Gideon went to war, there was a plan. He was instructed on the exact number of soldiers to take into battle and exact actions to take in battle (Judges chapter 6, 7 and 8).

For the prosperity of Egypt, during the seven years of famine, there was a plan. Joseph knew exactly the quantity of grain to save each year of plenty to cover the years of famine (Genesis 41:33-36)

A good plan is your blue print for success. If you do not have a plan for your life, then God cannot do anything with, through and for you. Without a plan, how can God commit resources into your hands? But with a plan, even God can trust you, to not only judiciously utilize His resources, but effectively render accounts.

David is another excellent example of a man who gave a lot of thoughts to his life and the work of God in his time, as we earlier alluded to in a previous chapter.

He had been notified by God that he would not build the temple; but, because of the great respect he had for the things of God, he had gone ahead to make provisions for the project which would be carried out long after he was gone (1 Chronicles 22:14-19).

Jesus told the disciples to watch and pray because His return would be unexpected. Like a thief in the night (Luke 12:39-40). With this in our mind, we should make the most of our time knowing we shall be held accountable for how our time is spent. To be able to give a proper account rendition of the time allotted to each and every one of us, we need to plan our days and life.

Dear child of God, it is possible even now, to have a plan for the next one thousand years, even while you maximize all of the resources available to you today (2 Peter 3:8).

> *The plans of the diligent lead surely to plenty, but those of everyone who is hasty, surely to poverty (Proverbs 21:5).*

It is important to note that there will be voices urging you to alter, modify or deviate from the plans you have made. Refuse to be distracted. When Lazarus was sick, Jesus did not respond immediately, that in itself was a plan. His plan was not to heal Lazarus but to demonstrate the resurrection power on him. Jesus went to Lazarus four days from the time of his death (John 11:17,38).

The disciples tried to urge Him to deviate from the plan, but He stayed on course. A lot of people would proffer well-meaning advice, suggestions, etc. Refuse to be distracted. Stay on course with the plan God has revealed to you.

The bible says, *"There is a way which seems right unto a man, but the end thereof are the ways of death"* (Proverbs 14:12).

The suggestions and advice you may receive from friends and well-meaning individuals, at face value may seem right, but is that what God has said concerning you specifically?

Forming Phase

Amos 3:3 asked a very pertinent question, *"Can two work together, unless they are agreed?"*
Do you want God involved in your business or project? For God Almighty to be interested or involved, your actionable plan has to be identical to the picture He has given you.

> *And see to it that you copy [exactly] their pattern which was shown you on the mountain (Exodus 25:40 AMP).*

When God created man, He physically formed man to look exactly like what He had created in the spirit, before breathing the breath of life into what He had formed. To effectively "stick to the pattern" or prototype received from God, you will need the ministry of the Holy Spirit, for it is He who will effectively teach you all things concerning the planning and implementation of your business plans.

A lot of people get frustrated, not because they did not hear from God at the onset, but because they were not able to effectively interpret what had been received, in the course of the implementation.

If I were to ask my five-year-old son to do a drawing of me, what he would reproduce, will be nothing close to what I look like. I can assure you. Why? Because he is still a child and unskilled. He will need growth, training and guidance from an expert to enable him effectively communicate an object or vision.

Even the great prophet and leader, Moses, messed up his first attempt in the execution of his ministry plan. He understood that he was called of God to deliver the children of Israel, but due to immaturity and inexperience, his first action ended in murder. In trying to deliver his people from oppression, he went about it the wrong way. He spent forty years in the wilderness, growing and maturing in his relationship with God, leading to a successful ministry. He learnt to get it right.

There is also the situation where the execution of the plan (timing, methodology, collaborations etc.) is on course. What is then required is persistence to achieve the desired results.

> *And He said to them, "Which of you shall have a friend, and go to him at **midnight** and say to him, 'Friend, lend me three loaves; for a friend of mine has come to me on his journey, and I have nothing to set before him'; and he will answer from within and say, 'Do not trouble me; the door is now shut, and my children are with me in bed; I cannot rise and give to you'? I say to you, though he will not rise and give to him because he is his friend, yet **because of his persistence** he will rise and give him as many as he needs" (Luke 11:5-8).*

Imagine if the man, due to the unfavorable response from his friend, had altered his plan. Probably waiting till morning to get the food. It would have defeated the purpose because his guest required food at that hour. As we see, his persistence paid off. What he did not get from his friend based on their relationship, he got on account of his persistence.

We also know of Moses, when he confronted Pharaoh. His request was declined ten times. He dug in his heels and persisted because he was confident that God was involved.

The result? The great exodus!!!!!

Set your face as a flint. Be dogged. Refuse to be moved.

The Holy Spirit – your Helper

Dear child of God, you must recognize and totally depend on the ministry of the Holy Spirit in your life. He is not just in your life to help you pray, or teach you the word of God. It is He who will give you the wisdom to take the right steps, not only in business, but in every sphere of your life.

John 15:26 describes the Holy Spirit as our comforter, advocate, intercessor, councilor, strengthener and standby. Everything you need to make your business or your project succeed, can only be through the ministry of the Holy Spirit. Therefore, cultivate a relationship with the Holy Spirit and learn to hear His voice. It is He that distinguishes you, like He did Daniel from every other person in the same line of work or business. He will make you an outstanding success.

The Phase of The Breath of Life

And the Lord God formed man of the dust of the ground, **and breathed into his nostrils the breath of life***, and man became a living being (Genesis 2:7).*

From the above scripture, we immediately recognize, that it was at the point when God breathed into man the breath of life, that he became living and active. So, you are done with the brooding phase (prayer and meditation), speaking and forming phase (writing and working the business plan).

CONGRATULATIONS!

Everything has come together. If you are into trade for instance, you have identified suitable vendors, done all the necessary negotiations, and received goods. In addition, you have probably paid for a shop space, fitted it adequately and the shop is ready for business.

At this point, it is like forming your business out of the dust of the ground. It brings to mind, the story of the dry bones in Ezekiel 37:7-10:

So I prophesied as I was commanded; and as I prophesied, there was a noise, and suddenly a rattling; and the bones came together, bone to bone. Indeed, as I looked, the sinews and the flesh came upon them, and the skin covered them over; but there was no breath in them. Also He said to me, "Prophesy to the breath, prophesy, son of man, and say to the breath, 'Thus says the Lord God: "Come from the four winds, O breath, and breathe on these slain, that they may live."'" So I prophesied as He commanded me, and breath came into them, and they lived, and stood upon their feet, an exceedingly great army.

A very familiar story indeed. God instructed Ezekiel to prophesy to bones that were very dry. And when he did, all the bones came together, flesh and skin covered them, but there was no breath in them.

Verse 10 tells us that, when breath came into them, they came to life and stood on their feet. If we have done everything according to God's purpose and leading, God will definitely honor and respond to our faith by bringing that business, ministry and work alive.

When there is the breath of life in your business, project or endeavor, it immediately places you head and shoulders above competition. Your brand can never conform or be subjected to the systems or principles of this world. Failure will never be an option. For when businesses are cast down, yours is lifted up above the floods of challenge, limitations, economic depression, recession, etc.

In Joshua chapter 6, God had a plan and strategy to give the Israelites victory over Jericho. When they adhered to the plan, Jericho was defeated. However, upon their victory over Jericho, Achan went against God's specific instruction by taking for himself, part of the loot from Jericho.

When Israel, subsequently engaged Ai in battle, they were sorely defeated, even though Ai was much smaller than Jericho. Why were they defeated? They had gone against God's instruction and He no longer was with them in battle.

We know of the story of Samson. He was to keep his head unshaven and remain a Nazirite (Judges 13:5). That was God's plan. As long as Samson kept to the plan, he was undefeated by the Philistines. The day he altered the plan, he became like an ordinary man and that subsequently led to his premature death.

Dear child of God, we cannot afford to cut corners in life. Stick to the original pattern and prototype given by the Spirit of God. When you do this, God becomes involved in your business and brand.

Living Phase

And the Lord God formed man of the dust of the ground, and breathed into his nostrils the breath of life; ***and man became a living being*** *(Genesis 2:7).*

To every life, there is a purpose. God is a God of predestination. God spoke to Jeremiah in Jeremiah 1:5 saying, *"Before I formed you in the womb I knew you; before you were born I sanctified you; I ordained you a prophet to the nations."*

Before you ever conceived or birthed that business or ministry or project, God had plans for it. He had something in mind for it. For us as Christians, it goes way beyond self fulfilment, profit, or running a successful business. God put life into that project or business or gift to bring glory to Himself.

A lot of Christians today get distracted by success itself. They are so busy running a profitable empire, handling mergers and acquisitions, enjoying business alliances and expansion that they forget the very reason God gave them the business or dream in the first place.

Please do not get me wrong. God is all for your growth, expansion and profitability.

Zechariah 1:17 says, *"My cities (the kingdom) shall again spread out through prosperity..."*

Whose prosperity was God referring to? Was it the prosperity of the nation you live or prosperity of the politicians? Absolutely not. God knows that His kingdom will only be spread through the prosperity of His children as we earlier said. So, God is interested, involved, and greatly supportive of your prosperity and success. That is why He is channeling so much good, expansion and profit to your business or ministry.

Dear child of God, do you recognize that, that business is for the glory of God? Are you seeing to it, in truth and deed, that it is actively involved in kingdom expansion?

The mistake a lot of Christians make, is when they begin to appropriate the good and the prosperity that God brings to them, for their selfish purposes.

The rich man in Luke 12:13-21 made a similar mistake. His business was thriving and making tremendous profit but all he could think of was self-aggrandization. The bible described him as a fool.

Why? Because he was misguided, and misappropriated his success. And sadly, that misappropriation, ended his life all together.

The bible has given us several examples of people who were misguided and ultimately met their destruction. These examples are given for us to learn from. Achan was another such example. When God gave Joshua and the people of Israel the people of Jericho, He also gave a caveat. The city and everything in it shall be destroyed as a tribute to the Lord and the treasures consecrated to the Lord. Nevertheless, Achan disregarded the Lord's instruction and kept some of the spoil for his personal gain, thus bringing disaster upon the whole nation of Israel. Generally speaking, it was not wrong to take spoils of war, but in this case, God had given a specific instruction against it (Joshua 6:19). Dear child of God, avoid selfish ambition.

Genesis 9:20-21 tells us that Noah, when he left the ark, began to be a farmer. He planted a vineyard which became successful. Unfortunately, however, he drank of the wine, was drunk, and became uncovered in his tent.

The error was not that Noah drank some of the wine, but that he allowed himself to become drunk. When one is drunk, he/she loses his identity, loses focus, and rational thoughts. Noah allowed himself to lose focus, and as a result, he became uncovered.

Dear child of God, when you lose your identity in "success" you become uncovered. You are no longer walking in agreement with God. You walk out of His protection, His covering, His provision and His glory.

> *He that diggeth a pit shall fall into it; and whoso breaketh an hedge, a serpent shall bite him (Ecclesiastes 10:8 KJV).*

Remember dear child of God, that we will give account. The servants with the five and the two talents, recognized that the money they received, did not belong to them. They just held them in trust for a certain period of time to make profit for the master. It is time to recognize that indeed God put life in that business for a purpose.

Rebuilding the Ruins

We understand from Genesis 26:15, that Abraham's servants dug wells in his time. Wells, in those days, were cardinal for lives' activities – cooking, drinking, bathing, watering the livestock, etc.

Everyone benefited from the wells in one way or the other. Sadly, after the death of Abraham, the wells were stopped by the Philistines, who filled them up with dirt. In other words, water supply was cut off and there was no human activity around the wells, because no

Phases of Execution

one benefited from them any longer. We can liken those wells today, to be the God-given dreams and purposes that we have been entrusted with for the furtherance of the kingdom - for nourishment, wellness and impacting the world with the water of God's word.

Sadly, as in the time of Abraham, there are enemies whose mission or purpose is to stop your wells. That is the state of a lot of businesses and ministries today, who had at the onset, flourished, thrived, were blessed, and were a blessing to people all over the world. Now, these enterprises are in ruins, abandoned, desolate and no longer blessing lives.

If this is your experience currently, I have good news for you. Even if the enemy may have shut down your dream, vision, ministry or work, the Holy Spirit has the capacity to raise it up again from the ruins.

Note that Isaac did not at first, try to dig new wells. He opened the wells of water that Abraham his father had dug, and even gave the wells the same names that his father had given them.

Dear child of God, it is time to reopen that well that has been stopped. Do not make the mistake of trying to look for what can work for you. Stick with God's plan and purpose for your life. Revisit the wells and open them.

Jesus in John 2:19-20 told the Jews, *"Destroy this temple, and in three days I will raise it up."* The Jews replied that it took forty-six years to build the temple, so how could Jesus raise it up in three days? Note the word *"destroy"* in verse 19. Jesus saying this, meant that even if the temple was in ruins, He would still raise it up in three days. He did, by the power of the Holy Spirit.

The state or level of the ruin, disorder or destruction of your ministry or work is immaterial. The question is, "Do you have the Holy Spirit?" If you do, no matter the time and resources it took to take that dream to that level of fulfilment, as you set to unstop those wells, you will realize that it will not be by your ability or speed, but by the speed, precision and power of the Holy Spirit.

That ministry will rise again. That dream or vision will come alive again. That business will come alive again by the speed of the Holy Spirit. And the glory of the latter shall far exceed that of the former, if you do not give up.

Dear child of God, note that God does not honor excuses. Usually excuses are justifications for failure, unproductivity or unfruitfulness. Do not give yourself a reason to slow down or stop. Keep moving. Never stop, and refuse to be stopped. Proverb 20:4 says, *"The lazy man will not plow because of winter; he will beg during harvest and have nothing."*

Chapter Twelve

Dealing with Delays

For the vision is yet for an appointed time; but at the end it will speak, and it will not lie. Though it tarries, wait for it; because it will surely come, it will not tarry.
—Habakkuk 2:3

For optimal effectiveness in ministry or in your secular work, we have underscored the importance of training, training, and training again. Indeed, training generally enables you to develop competencies, strength and skill, but as a Christian, training goes over and beyond that because God and kingdom expansion are involved. Consequently, besides building competencies and skill, God expects you to develop your spirit man because, essentially the work you do, whether it be ministry or secular is spiritual.

The bible says in 1 Timothy 4:8, *"For physical training is of some value (useful for a little), but godliness (spiritual training) is useful and of value in everything and in every way, for it holds promise for the present life and also for the life which is to come" (AMP).* Physical training in the above scripture, comprises not only bodily training, but training of the intellect, emotions, skill, competencies, etc. We understand that all of this is good and of some value, but what counts most, is the spiritual training because as the bible says, *"Godliness (spiritual training) is useful and of value in everything and in every way."* This means it is important in your work life whether ministry or secular.

A lot of Christians have wrongly placed so much more emphasis on physical training, with little or no attention to training in godliness. It is erroneous to think or conclude that godliness does not really matter in the work place, probably because it is not a KPI (Key Performance Indicator). To God, who is your chief employer, it is a critical ingredient for success in every area of life especially in the work environment.

Let us take a look at the journey of the children of Israel to the promised land. That journey in God's original plan, was expected to be concluded in a couple of days, but the journey took forty long years. And in those forty long years, a lot of people lost their lives.

Dealing with Delays

Was God wicked? Why would He allow His people to wander aimlessly in the wilderness?

God was not satisfied with the state of their heart towards Him – they walked in unbelief, they murmured, they complained, they got drunk, they were immoral, and they followed other gods. They sought to worship God on their own terms.

From a natural view point, all of these deficiencies should not have prevented Israel from subduing hostile territory, but for God, the ability to drive out their enemies and take up cities, was not directly dependent on their strength in numbers or experience in battle, but the state of their heart.

> *But you shall hold fast to the Lord your God, as you have done to this day. For the Lord has driven out from before you great and strong nations; but as for you, no one has been able to stand against you to this day. One man of you shall chase a thousand, for the Lord your God is He who fights for you, as He promised you (Joshua 23:8-10).*

Dear child of God, are you experiencing an unexplainable delay in the actualization of God's promise concerning you and your work? You have done all the necessary trainings, obtained all the required certification, secured excellent trade agreement (where necessary or where applicable) and yet you struggle.

The Lord may just be trying to get your attention on a very important aspect of training, that you may have missed out – training in godliness. You may say, "But I am a Christian and I pray every morning before leaving my house." That is not enough. God wants you to develop certain spiritual qualities and competencies that will see you through life and work even "when the arm of flesh" fails.

Every physical training requires investment in time, focus, discipline, attention, and spiritual training demands no less. Go back to God. There are secrets to life and secrets to that specific work that you do that He wants to teach you (Psalm 25:14).

Sadly, if you still think spiritual training does not matter to be a success in your work place, you may have a similar experience to what the children of Israel had, going around in circles. This experience can be very frustrating and disconcerting, and yet God wants you to have a life of sweat less (without struggle) prosperity.

> *But the path of the just is as the shining light, that shineth more and more unto the perfect day (Proverb 4:18 KJV).*

Dear child God, if your current experience is not as Proverb 4:18 above describes – a life of consistent progress and productivity, then check it. You may very well have little or inadequate spiritual training to tide you over in work and life. God is saying to you as He said in Deuteronomy 2:3 (NET), *"You have circled around this mountain long enough; now turn north."*

This is the time! GET UP. GET TRAINED. MOVE FORWARD.

Delays as a Result of Collaboration

We know the story of Joshua and Caleb in Numbers 14:26-38. They were sent in a delegate of twelve men, to survey the land of Jericho. Out of all the twelve men, only Joshua and Caleb came back with a good report.

On account of this, the bible records that, God determined that only Joshua and Caleb, of their generation would enter the promised land. Consequently, all the contemporaries of Moses, Joshua and Caleb died, leaving only Joshua, Caleb and the children of their contemporaries.

It took forty long years for that particular generation to be wiped out, and the children to grow and mature enough to take possession of the promised land, thus increasing the wait time for Joshua and Caleb (in whom God delighted in), for the said forty years.

Living Out God's Purpose and Plan

The two men, even if they wanted to, could not break out from the nation of Israel, to take possession of the land of promise.

Similarly, you may find yourself in a particular ministry or work environment, and may be affected by God's decision or workings in that environment.

God's promise may be tied to the entire group, and since every Christian does not peak spiritual training and maturity at the same time; you as an individual, may be affected by the delay of the entire group in actualizing God's promise. In a situation like this, be careful to keep up with the right attitude and not be sucked into complaining, murmuring and unbelief.

> *And now, behold, the Lord has kept me alive, as He said, these forty-five years, ever since the Lord spoke this word to Moses while Israel wandered in the wilderness; and now, here I am this day, eighty-five years old. As yet I am as strong this day as on the day that Moses sent me; just as my strength was then, so now is my strength for war, both for going out and for coming in (Joshua 14:10-11).*

In the text above, Caleb commented that he had had to wait forty years, from when God gave the promise to Moses. Imagine experiencing a delay of forty years, that you personally had nothing to do with. Indeed, it is a great trial to any man's patience and endurance. Caleb maintained the right attitude concerning the promise, and unwavering devotion to God throughout the forty long years. This was evidenced in verse 11, *"As yet I am as strong this day as on the day that Moses sent me; just as my strength was then, so now is my strength for war, both for going out and for coming in."*

This was a man who did not allow circumstances to determine his devotion and service. In verse 10, we see that he was ready, even at eighty-five years, to do whatever God required him to do – which would even include fighting side by side with the children or subordinates of his contemporaries.

This speaks of great humility, which will be handled in the next chapter.

Dear child of God, can you be another Caleb in that ministry or work place, living an exemplary life of humility, perseverance, and devotion to God, in spite of the circumstances?

> *Therefore, as the elect of God, holy and dearly loved, clothe yourselves with a heart of mercy, kindness, humility, gentleness,*

> *and patience, bearing with one another and forgiving one another, if someone happens to have a complaint against anyone else. Just as the Lord has forgiven you, so you also forgive others. And to all these virtues add love, which is the perfect bond (Colossians 3:12-14 NET).*

Fear-Induced Delay

Fear paralyses and immobilizes. The children of Israel experienced this paralyzing fear when they were helmed in, between the red sea and the Egyptian army.

Moses cried out to God and God responded, *"Why do you cry unto Me? tell the children of Israel to go forward"* (Exodus 14:15). One can describe this situation as being at your wit's end. You have done everything you know to do, and yet there seems to be no way out of the predicament.

A lot of Christians today are paralyzed by the hopelessness of fear. All options of prayer, fasting, seed sowing have been explored and yet nothing! In this situation, all physical trainings seem to fail, and only the training in godliness can yield to you, the secret or password that can make you overcome. It is not about employing what you know at this time. Like

Moses, he did what was second nature to him, he cried out to God, but at that time, that was not what was required, for God asked him, *"Why do you cry unto me?"* (this is not the time). God gave Moses a strategy and that was all that was needed.

Indeed, the secret of the Lord (to overcome, breakthrough, excel, go forward) is with them that fear Him (Psalm 25:14). There is a time for everything under the sun. So, there is a time and place for prayer. Prayer is good, but a lot of Christians have tried to put God into a stereotype of prayer and fasting.

God is very dynamic. Jesus in Matthew 17:21, made a note that a particular challenge, could only go by prayer and fasting. This implies that prayer and fasting may not be required for all challenges. At other times, strategy, fast thinking, quick actions will be required.

Dear child of God, it is so important to have the right balance of physical training and spiritual training. Furnished with both trainings, you are set to be a victor for life. When you find yourself helmed in, simply ask the Lord the strategy out of that situation, and He will give it to you.

Gaining Strength in Periods of Delay

It is not your circumstances that define you, but what you do in, with and about your circumstances that ultimately define you, and determine your trajectory to greatness. Whether the period of delay you are experiencing is of your own making or not, what you do in this time matters a great deal, because it will definitely determine your outcome.

David had a promise of the throne of Israel but had to go through a long period of waiting, hallmarked by building survival instincts and skills as well as leadership abilities. He maintained the right attitude throughout his waiting time, and when he finally ascended the throne, all of the lessons he had learnt, helped him reign successfully as a king, and as a warrior who never lost a battle.

The same can be said about Joseph. He could have murmured and complained, but through humility, he strengthened his gift of interpreting dreams through use, while in prison. He also learned administrative skills both as a prisoner and as a servant in Potiphar's house. This ultimately secured for him the highly esteemed position of Prime Minister in Egypt, at which he demonstrated great leadership abilities and business acumen.

Dear child of God, use your waiting time rightly. There is something to be learned, acquired and earned in this period, that will make you outstanding in ministry and in your work environment.

Seest thou a man diligent in his business? he shall stand before kings; he shall not stand before mean men (Prov 22:29 KJV).

Chapter Thirteen

Humility: The Path to Greatness

Before destruction the heart of a man is haughty, and before honor is humility.
— Proverbs 18:12

In the journey of life, humility is key. No matter the degree of your success or achievements in life, it is important to stay humble.

For some people, pride plays out at the onset of life's journey, probably because of pedigree, background, privileges and entitlements of birth, while for others, it shows up when they begin to experience a certain level of success or accomplishments.

Humility is a virtue, a way of life that God respects.

1 Peter 5:5 urges us to *'Be clothed with humility, for "**God resists the proud**, but gives grace to the humble."'*

Peter gave this instruction, not to unbelievers but to God's elects (Christians). And from the scripture, we see that God Himself resists the Christian who is proud. What does the word "resist" mean in this context? Fight, attack, repel, counterattack, oppose, battle.

If you exhibit pride in life, God Himself resists you. It is a sorry state for a man, whom God is pitted against. You cannot win in any endeavor. Sometimes, when things do not seem to be going well in life, business and family, in spite of having done all the right things, check it. God Himself may be resisting you because of pride.

Even now, reflect on your relationship with your colleagues, staff, employees or bosses. Do you disdain instruction and correction? Do you rebel against constituted authority? Are you callous, insensitive and proud? If you have observed the slightest hint of pride, in any of these areas, take very urgent steps to work on yourself.

On the subject of humility, we will look closely at three characters – Joseph, Paul and Moses.

Paul

Paul was a learned man who understood the law and knew his rights. On an occasion, while being questioned by the high priest Ananias, the same high priest instructed that he be slapped. This act was against the law, and Paul reacted against it vehemently.

When reproved by bystanders, concerning the way he spoke to the high priest, Paul responded that he did not realize that Ananias was the high priest. He understood that though Ananias was wrong, Paul himself was also wrong for speaking against the office of the high priest (Acts 23:1-5).

Dear child of God, it does not matter if your boss (in ministry or secular work), is wrong in his treatment of you or in the decisions he makes. Respect the office, because that authority/office is constituted by God (Romans 13:1-7).

Instead of being rebellious, arrogant and rude, pray for your boss, and God will give you wisdom in your relationship with him or her (1 Timothy 2:1-4). Even in that unpleasant situation, there is something of value to learn.

Joseph

From the story of Joseph, we understand that he enjoyed certain privileges and entitlements, that even his siblings did not have, being the love of his father's life. In today's parlance, we could say, that Joseph had a pampered upbringing.

Shortly after, due to the treachery of his siblings, he was forced into a life that was completely foreign to him and infra dig. He became a servant in Potiphar's house, and then a prisoner. He could have easily developed a wrong attitude, being unused to this base existence, but rather he remained humble, serving with quiet dignity and respect, both in Potiphar's house and in prison.

If for any reason, he had exhibited pride due to his circumstance, he would not have gone far in life. Because he stayed humble, he was able to learn skills that prepared him for the greatness he had dreamt about.

Moses

Moses was the youngest of his siblings and yet he was given the tremendous responsibility of leading the children of Israel out of Egypt and into the promised land. A responsibility he carried with great humility.

Numbers 23:3 described Moses *"As very humble, more than all men who were on the face of the earth."*

God showed great respect for this strength in character. At some point, his siblings Miriam and Aaron did not agree with a decision he made in his personal life, and spoke against him (probably because of their age advantage). God rose in Moses' defense, and in His anger punished his sister Miriam. If you stay humble, in spite of injustice or wrong done against you by the people you work with, God Himself will rise in your defense, honor and promote you.

Dear child of God, stop pride before it stops you. Pride robs you of true greatness, while humility brings about speedy attainment of greatness.

God gives grace to the humble (1 Peter 5:5).

Humility Pays

A point to note is, there is no status of maturity or fulness in humility. So, you cannot assume that you have reached a certain level of humility in life, therefore the time has come for you to be promoted.

It is God who decides the time and nature of your exaltation or promotion. Your part is to stay humble.

> *Then you will have glory in the presence of those who sit at the table with you. For whoever exalts himself will be humbled,*

> *and he who humbles himself will be exalted (Luke 14:11).*

Humility pays. The glory and honor from God come through the path of humility. It is not self-imposed or something to be grasped. David was already chosen by God, and anointed king of Israel, long before the reigning king, Saul, died. At Saul's death, the throne was eventually vacant. Though David knew that this was the throne he was anointed for, did not make a grab at it but waited to be "fetched" by the men of the land (2 Samuel 2:4;5:1-5). That is humility.

God will always reward humility.

Philippians 2:9 says, *"For this reason also (because He obeyed and so completely humbled himself) God has highly exalted him and bestowed on him the name which is above every name..."* (AMP).

The above scripture refers to our Lord Jesus Christ. Even He, through obedience and humility, was highly exalted by the Father. If Jesus, who is our perfect example, earned His glory and reputation through humility, what makes you think you will gain yours by other means?

Dealing with Pride as a Minister

Over time, I have heard ministers testify about what God did through them – healings and other miracles. Be careful. There is a very thin line between giving the glory to God for testimonies, and appropriating the glory for yourself, as a minister.

Sadly, a lot of ministers today, have crossed that line, probably in the hope of converting a soul into his local assembly.

When we look at the practical examples of Jesus, as He healed and worked miracles, we observe the following:

1. **Jesus consistently drew attention to the role of the person's faith in the specific miracle**

   "...your faith has made you well" (Matthew 9:22).

   "according to your faith let it be to you" (Matthew 9:29).

   "...great is your faith! Let it be to you as you desire" (Matthew 15:28).

By doing this, He did not draw attention to Himself, as the healer, but redirected the focus of the people to faith in the God who heals.

As a minister, no matter how anointed you are, be careful to redirect the trust, dependency and faith of the people to God and His word.

A lot of pastors today, are literally given the honor, praise and adulation due God, by members of their congregation.

Acts 14:8-20 tells the story of a lame man who received healing as he listened to Paul's teaching. The crowd was ecstatic in their joy and excitement, and labelled Paul and Barnabas gods. They were so intent on their worship of these two men, based on the miracle they witnessed, that the priest of their temple brought oxen and garlands to sacrifice to Paul and Barnabas.

It may not be this dramatic in our time today, but believe me, a lot of ministries have moved the focus of their love and faith from God to the pastor.

I am not saying that ministers are not deserving of love and honor by the congregation, they do (1 Thessalonians 5:12-13), but be careful that as a minister you have not assumed the place of God in the eyes of your brethren.

Just as Paul and Barnabas reacted vocally and earnestly against the hero worship at that time, speak out and condemn any action from the congregation, that appropriates the glory due God to you.

In addition, be careful that the testimonies you give are centered on God's ability and love, and do not become a recitation of your personal achievements in ministry.

2. Jesus avoided crowds initiating His exaltation

After one of His more popular miracles of feeding the five thousand, the people decided that He was the right prophet and leader. They decided to take Him by force and make Him king. Jesus perceived this intent before they were able to execute it, and tactfully withdrew (John 6:14-15).

You may be a junior minster or an assistant pastor, probably doing greater exploits than your mentor or boss. People whom you have blessed and impacted may tend to nudge you or incite you to make a grab for an exalted position. This is not God at work. Be careful. Be spiritually alert and discerning at all times, to enable you retract tactfully like Jesus did. That is humility.

3. Jesus hardly talked about past miracles

You will observe that Jesus hardly talked about miracles He had performed in other towns or cities.

The current works or miracles that He did wherever He was, spoke of the Father that worked in Him.

Jesus Himself speaking said, *"The very works that I do bear witness of Me, that the Father has sent Me"* (John 5:36).

Let us look at this scripture closely. *"The very works that I do."* This was said in the present continuous tense. Note He did not say, the very works that I did. He did not live in the past, but He lived and operated in the "now faith." As a result, signs and miracles accompanied Him, and bore witness of Him wherever He went.

Also, let us look at still a part of that scripture *"bear witness of Me, that the Father has sent Me."* The miracles that Jesus performed, always pointed to the Father and not to Him even though He is in truth, God.

Dear minister, pride is subtle and usually creeps in undetected. Be very clear of the intention of the testimony you give. It should not be to bring members to your ministry, but to stir faith in the God who has sent you. Therefore, dear minister, I leave you with this gentle reminder as seen in 2 Corinthians 3:5:

> *Not that we are fit (qualified and sufficient in ability) of ourselves to form personal judgments or to claim or count anything as*

coming from us, but our power and ability and sufficiency are from God (AMP).

The Conclusion in Humility

In carrying out any responsibility in the course of ministry or secular work, the very first requirement is to lose your identity. Making yourself of no reputation.

That is not a state or experience that a lot of people will jump at, but that is the very first step to greatness.

We will look closely at our perfect example in Philippians 2:5-7:

> *Let this same attitude and purpose and [humble] mind be in you which was in Christ Jesus: [Let Him be your example in humility:] Who, although being essentially one with God and in the form of God [possessing the fullness of the attributes which make God God], did not think this equality with God was a thing to be eagerly grasped or retained, But stripped Himself [of all privileges and rightful dignity], so as to assume the guise of a servant (slave), in*

> *that He became like men and was born a human being (AMP).*

The above scriptures show clearly that Jesus is God, one with God, possessing the fullness of all the divine attributes or the entire nature of deity. However, He did not see this oneness with God, as something to be asserted.

Verse 7, tells us that it was not God the Father that stripped Him of His privileges and rightful dignity, due Him as God. Jesus Himself, emptied/stripped Himself of every privilege, making Himself of no reputation at all.

Jesus could never have successfully made that journey to the cross, and to the grave, if He did not first put aside the privileges of His exalted position.

Similarly, in fulfilling purpose, you will, of necessity, have to put aside your privileges or entitlements. Never feel too important, too connected, too highly placed to bring yourself down to the level of humility in service. We have seen leaders who struggle in leadership and are disconnected from their subjects, simply because they have not emptied themselves.

You cannot serve, as a leader, with a full tank.

Dear child of God, in your place of service, have you stripped yourself? Have you emptied yourself or are you still asserting your qualifications, achievements, self-respect, seniority, etc. in the line of duty?

If you are still bothered about whether you are being accorded the respect due your office, then you have not started the journey of service in humility. Put aside all esteem, entitlements, reputation, and accomplishments, to enable you be effective in service unto God.

No one said it is an easy decision, but it is a necessary one to greatness. So dear child of God, we have been given a perfect example, may be not pleasant example, but it behooves us to follow through on this example in humility.

> *"Let this same attitude and purpose and [humble] mind be in you which was in Christ Jesus: [Let Him be your example in humility:]"*

Chapter Fourteen

The Role of Prayer

*Then He spoke a parable to them,
that men always ought to pray and
not lose heart.*
— Luke 18:1

Jesus, while physically on earth, lived a very successful life and had a very successful ministry because He understood the importance of prayer. We all know that whether in relationship, marriage, ministry or business, communication is probably one of the most important activities in life.

Without effective communication, nothing in life can thrive or be sustained. Prayer is essentially the effective communication between man and God.

Though Jesus was (and is) the Son of God, He did not take prayer for granted. He understood prayer as an effective communication with the Father.

The bible says concerning Jesus that, *"...in the morning, rising up a great while before day, He went out and departed into a solitary place, and there prayed"* (Mark 1:35).

On another occasion, it was recorded that He prayed all night (Luke 6:12). Little wonder Jesus was such a tremendous success. He did nothing of Himself. Through prayer, He was in total sync with the Father.

Dear child of God, in your life, work or ministry, is prayer a priority? Does it have a time and place in your life?

Looking closely at the ministry of Jesus, we quickly see that He led a very busy life. He was in very high demand by people in His immediate environs and beyond. He always, deliberately and with great discipline, gave time to prayer. Sadly, a lot of Christians today, are reeling out excuses on a daily basis, why they cannot maintain an effective prayer life. They appear overwhelmed with the demands of life, family and work, neglecting the very thing meant to guarantee a rich and productive life for them.

I mentioned earlier that I had been a banker for several years. We all know that the banking sector is an extremely demanding one. It would have been so easy for me to be sucked into the pressures of work and family, leaving no time for prayer. I ensured that my prayer life and personal fellowship with God did not suffer in any way. This habit and discipline gave me clarity of purpose, direction, and precision in carrying out all of my daily tasks and responsibilities, both at home and at work. You cannot win without prayer.

It is amazing that today, there are pastors who are so caught up in the business of running a church or ministry, that they forget to have a rich and fulfilling personal fellowship with God.

There is no excuse for you, whether you are a doctor, banker, engineer or minister. God has given you 24 hours in a day. Invest them wisely and make prayer a priority.

We know the story of the two sisters: Mary and Martha, who both loved Jesus and had a relationship with Him.

When Jesus came into their home, the bible records that it was actually Martha who welcomed Jesus into the home. She was very busy and distracted *"with much serving..."* (Luke 10:38-42). Martha was not busy catering to herself. She was not busy washing her clothes or taking care of her personal needs. The bible described that she was very busy with her serving responsibilities in Jesus' honor. Note the word *"serving."* She understood that serving Jesus was a responsibility for her. The problem with the degree of her involvement with the service, was that it became a distraction in itself. A distraction from spending time communing, and enjoying fellowship and intimacy with Jesus.

That is the state of so many Christians in ministry and secular work. They have become so busy with and distracted by the work, that prayer and fellowship have become redundant.

In verse 40 to 42, Martha had complained about her sister's unwillingness to serve and Jesus' response to her was, *"Martha, Martha you are worried and bothered and anxious about so many things, but only one thing is necessary, for Mary has chosen the good part..."*

What Jesus said to Martha, He is saying to us all. Dear child of God, only one thing is necessary... which is your personal relationship and fellowship with the Master. This does not exclude the importance or necessity of other activities in life, but this is the anchor that holds together every other area. It is also the fuel that will keep you over and above in every other area of life.

Ministering to the Lord

As they ministered to the Lord and fasted, the Holy Spirit said... (Acts 13:2).

Note that the Spirit spoke, after they had ministered to the Lord in the above scripture. Ministering to the Lord is the essence of worship. You will never know the depth in the Spirit, or experience the supernatural, beyond the ordinary, until you start ministering to the Lord.

Many Christians wonder why their lives and work seem so dull and ordinary. They do not experience the power of God as they should. The problem, for the most part, lies in this area of prayer.

When you fellowship with the Lord, you activate the ministry of the Holy Spirit in your life. He will teach, lead and direct you; ushering in the supernatural into your work, life and ministry.

Prayer Makes Power Available

But you shall receive power when the Holy Spirit has come upon you... (Acts 1:8).

No doubt as a Christian, you have the Holy Spirit, so you have access to this power referred to, in the above scripture. However, having access to this power alone, does not guarantee its availability.

For example, you can be present with someone, but not available to that person. It is like a man, who, though he is in the house, is not available to his wife. He is probably in the living room reading a newspaper. His wife is talking to him but he is not listening; he is present with her but not available to her. This lets us know that being present or having access to is not the same as being available. To be available, is to have your attention and cooperation.

The question is, "So, how does one make the power available?" Let us take a look at James 5:16, *"...the earnest (heartfelt, continued) prayer of the righteous man makes tremendous power available..."* (AMP).

Dear child of God, the prayer referred to here is not the hurried prayer you do at your dinner table, or while rushing to work. Matthew 6:6 describes the kind of prayer involved here:

> *But you, when you pray, go into your room, and when you have shut your door, pray to your Father who is in the secret place; and your Father who sees in secret will reward you openly.*

It is done with so much passion and emotion, and for that reason, you may have to separate yourself from everybody. This kind of prayer produces results. Elijah was another man who prayed like this. On an occasion, he prayed that there will be no rain, and the earth went without rain for three and half years. He prayed again, and the heaven supplied rain. How was he able to do it? The answer lies in book of James again:

The Role of Prayer

*Elijah was a man with a nature like ours, and **he prayed earnestly** that it would not rain; and it did not rain on the land for three years and six months (James 5:17).*

He prayed earnestly. Some good definitions for the word earnest are, to be intent and direct in purpose, to be zealous or fervent, marked by a deep feeling of conviction. The bible says it is heartfelt and continued. You do not just pray it once and stop. You continue seriously and earnestly, with a deep feeling of conviction, until you get the note of victory in your spirit.

Jesus prayed like this, many times. No wonder the power of God was always available to Him throughout His earthly ministry. Sadly, today, not very many people pray this way, but many expect to get the kind of results that Jesus and Elijah got. You need to learn how to pray earnestly in private, so that you can have the power of the Holy Spirit working on your behalf publicly.

In spite of work demands or life's challenges and pressures, sct yourself to pray like Jesus often – privately, earnestly, fervently, passionately and intensely. Make this a practice, a lifestyle; and watch yourself, family, career and ministry move from one level of glory to another, as you walk in the supernatural everyday of your life.

The Responsibility of Prayer

At the onset of this chapter on prayer, we established that prayer is an effective communication with the Father.

1 Corinthians 1:9 tells us, *"God is faithful by whom you were called unto the fellowship of the Son Jesus Christ our Lord."*

From this scripture, we see that we have been called into companionship with Jesus Christ our Lord. Prayer is first and foremost, a fellowship with our Heavenly Father, but it is also a responsibility.

> *Never stop praying, especially for others... Stay alert and keep praying for God's people (Ephesians 6:18 CEV).*

We have a responsibility as Christians, to ensure that whatever changes we seek in our lives; work, home, ministry are effected. One of the ways we do this is through prayer.

A lot of people blame God when things go wrong. They make statements like, "If God did not want that thing to happen, why did He let it happen?" Remember the two sisters we talked about, Mary and Martha. They indirectly blamed Jesus for their brother's death

The Role of Prayer

saying, "If You had been here, Lazarus would not have died" (John 11:21, 32).

Dear child of God, it is important to remind us that the authority to establish the will of God on earth, and keep the devil and his demons under our feet has been delegated to us: *"Your kingdom come. Your will be done on earth as it is in heaven"* (Luke 11:2).

In other words, evil prevails when good men do nothing (do not pray).

The bible gives us an example of the consequences of not taking up the responsibility of prayer, whatever your calling. James, the brother of John, was arrested by Herod during the persecution of the early church. Perhaps, the brethren were thinking, "Herod does not know the anointing on brother James; he will be out of prison in no time," so they did nothing (did not pray). While they were still there believing in the anointing of brother James, someone rushed in with the news, brother James had been killed. (Acts 12:2).

Understand that James was no ordinary disciple. He was one of the three closest disciples to Jesus.

While the brethren were reeling with the shock of the news, and wondering why Jesus did not do something, another bad news came, that Peter has been arrested. Thank God, this time around, they realized they had a responsibility to pray.

> *Peter was therefore kept in prison, but constant prayer was offered to God for him by the church (Acts 12:5).*

As they prayed, Peter was miraculously set free by an angel.

> *Now behold, an angel of the Lord stood by him, and a light shone in the prison; and he struck Peter on the side and raised him up, saying, "Arise quickly!" And his chains fell off his hands (Acts 12:7).*

If only they had taken their responsibility serious at first, probably James would not have been killed.

Dear child of God, be wise. Do not take anything in your life – family, business, work or ministry for granted. You do not have to wait for evil to strike: for the landlord to give you a quit notice, for your staff or business associate to defraud you, for your goods to be seized by the authorities, before you learn to pray. Avert the evil. Take up your responsibility of prayer and cause changes in the name of Jesus.

Prayer of Praise and Thanksgiving

You also, as living stones, are being built up a spiritual house, a holy priesthood, to offer up spiritual sacrifices acceptable to God through Jesus Christ (1 Peter 2:5).

The above scripture talks about offering up spiritual sacrifices. Just what are these sacrifices? Hebrew 13:15, informs us that these sacrifices are the fruit of our lips.

Just as the priests offered sacrifices of burnt offerings and burnt incense in the old testament, we in the new testament offer sacrifices of praise to God with our words.

The sacrifices of praise are the confessions, declarations, psalms, hymns and spiritual songs of the glory, grace and goodness of God that we make unto Him.

As you do this, you send forth incense unto God (Revelations 5:7;8:2-3).

Anybody can pray, but it takes the child of God to send forth incense by the Spirit, into the presence of God.

Too many times, people associate prayer with problem solving. When things do not go right or as expected, you feel the need or urge to pray. This is wrong. Ideally, you do not need to have a problem to pray.

Prayer is a ministry for us as new testament believers. You do not wait to be happy to praise God, or only when He has answered a prayer. In the midst of challenges and troubles, is the best time to praise God.

The bible talks about the sacrifice of praise. Given that it is a sacrifice, it may not always be a pleasant experience. So even when your heart is heavy, learn to praise.

Another example to learn from, is the story of Paul and Silas. These two gentlemen were fervent in doing God's work. In the course of their work, they were attacked by the crowd, stripped and severely flogged with rods. They were arrested and put in the inner cell, with their feet fastened in the stocks. This was a very bleak situation indeed, but instead of murmuring, crying or questioning God; Paul and Silas were praying and singing hymns to God. The bible records that suddenly, there was a violent earthquake, the foundation of the prison was shaken. All the prison doors were opened, and everyone's chains came loose (Acts 16:25-26).

Praise releases power that overwhelms every situation or circumstance.

In the course of your work and ministry, make praise a habit. Praise is guaranteed to shake the very foundations of every adverse situation and challenge you may be experiencing.

So dear child of God, do you desire to work in perpetual victory and triumph in work and ministry? PRAISE!

> *Rejoice always, pray without ceasing, in everything give thanks; for this is the will of God in Christ Jesus for you (1 Thessalonians 5:16-18).*

Conclusion

Dear child of God, we have traversed fourteen chapters, in which the Spirit of God has communicated expressly. The main thrust of this book is on finding our purpose as Christians and children of God, and being productive in that purpose.

I am confident that you have been as richly blessed as I have been, with the richness of God's wisdom and clarity of God's purpose for us.

Remember that you are expected to be productive in your given area of endeavor or ministry. God has lavished on you all the grace and resources required to succeed in life. So, from God's point of view, you are without excuse.

Personally, as I wrote this book, I perceived in my spirit that this book is the onset of my own success story, because I dared to say "yes" to God's specific leading in writing, against all odds.

This book indeed is a testament to God's unwavering commitment to any child of God, when he or she acts in complete and total obedience to God.

The teachings contained in this book are guaranteed to steer you on the right course, keep you on course and keep you productive and successful in life.

Regardless of where you are right now, follow God's instructions and teachings in this manual. It has the ability to make you, as it has made me.

It is my prayer that through this book, you shall experience tremendous success in every area of life, and you shall impact your world forever.

Welcome to the beginning of the rest of your life!

Get Connected

This book may mean nothing to you if you do not know the giver of life and purpose. To unlock your God given potentials and be truly successful in life, you need to have a relationship with the Lord Jesus, who paid the ultimate sacrifice for your life. I therefore invite you to make Jesus Christ the Lord of your life by praying thus:

Oh Lord God, I believe with all my heart in Jesus Christ, Son of the living God. I believe He died for me and God raised Him from the dead. I believe He is alive today. I confess with my mouth that Jesus Christ is the Lord of my life, from this day. Through Him and His name, I have eternal life. I am born again. I am now a child of God. Hallelujah.

> *Because if you acknowledge and confess with your lips that Jesus is Lord and in your heart believe (adhere to, trust in, and rely on the truth) that God raised Him from the dead, you will be saved. For with the heart a person believes (adheres to, trusts in, and*

relies on Christ) and so is justified (declared righteous, acceptable to God), and with the mouth he confesses (declares openly and speaks out freely his faith) and confirms [his] salvation. The Scripture says, no man who believes in Him [who adheres to, relies on, and trusts in Him] will [ever] be put to shame or be disappointed (Romans 10:9-11 AMP).

Congratulations! You have begun a journey of purpose and fulfillment in Christ Jesus.

Printed in Great Britain
by Amazon